Small Spaces

Small Spaces

MAXIMIZING LIMITED SPACES FOR LIVING

Elizabeth Wilhide

jacqui
small

First published in 2008 by Jacqui Small LLP,
7 Greenland Street, London NW1 0ND

Text copyright © Elizabeth Wilhide 2008
Photography, design and layout copyright
© Jacqui Small 2008

The author's moral rights have been asserted.

PUBLISHER Jacqui Small
EDITORIAL MANAGER Lesley Felce
DESIGNER Maggie Town
EDITOR Sian Parkhouse
PICTURE RESEARCHER Nadine Bazar
PRODUCTION Peter Colley

ISBN 978 1 906417 15 4

A catalogue record for this book is
available from the British Library.

2010 2009 2008
10 9 8 7 6 5 4 3 2 1

Printed in China

contents

Small space living can be something to celebrate. It doesn't have to mean settling for second best. Increasingly these days, it's a positive choice for many of us and for all sorts of reasons that are not simply to do with keeping the mortgage manageable, though staying within one's budget is always a good idea to maintain peace of mind.

You only have to think of the advantages. Small spaces are easier and more economical to run – you will save time, effort and money. At the same time, because you are dealing with relatively limited surface areas, you will be able to afford better materials and detailing. Most importantly, small space living concentrates the mind. When you haven't a great deal of room to play with, you have to be selective and focused and this is no bad thing.

To make the most of the space at your disposal requires careful consideration and sometimes a special approach or sideways leap. Thorough planning will help ensure your home functions smoothly and efficiently and accommodates the way you want to live. Clever design strategies will win you more floor area and better spatial quality. And, in terms of decoration, there are tried and tested ways of making a small space seem bigger without compromising your personal style.

Elizabeth Wilhide

OPPOSITE TOP Many small spaces, particularly in converted buildings, are awkwardly shaped. Placing a bed so that the head lies against a sloping wall is a good use of space.

OPPOSITE BELOW Structural columns and beams help to define separate areas in an open-plan space, making a visual distinction between the kitchen and eating area.

THIS PAGE Small space living doesn't have to be short on style. A Venetian mirror and marble worktop and splashback add a touch of glamour to a tiny kitchen and its adjoining bathroom.

Design Strategies

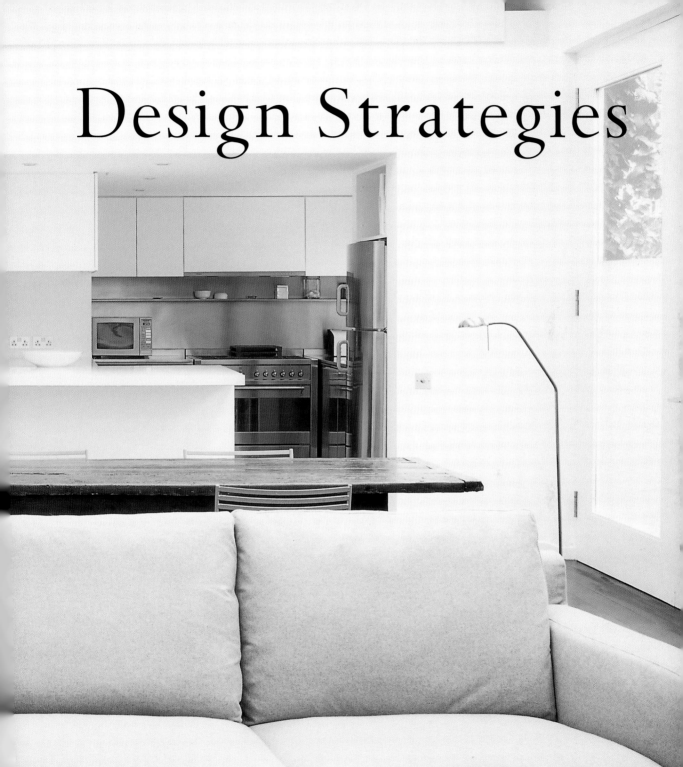

First things first: know your home.

Small space living means that every centimetre counts. An essential part of the planning process is working out exactly how much space you have and how it is arranged so you can think about ways of improving it. Good small space design is holistic, not piecemeal. To help yourself get a grip on the big picture, it is worth taking detailed measurements of every area and making a sketch plan, marking on details and features such as windows and where power points are located. Such plans are not only good visual aids, they can also form a useful role in preliminary discussions with professionals such as architects, or when you are planning a new kitchen or bathroom and consulting an in-store design service. Always work to scale.

The next step is to work out where your priorities lie. What is more important to you – having a garden or entertaining, a generous kitchen or a home office? Where floor area is limited there may be the need for a certain amount of doubling up, which often means building in flexibility so that different activities can be accommodated within the same multipurpose area.

Sometimes the way to make the most of a small space is by taking direct action: spatial changes that entail taking down or moving walls, creating new openings or adjusting partitions. This section is all about getting the basic structure right so your home works hard for you.

TOP LEFT Metal concertina folding stairs provide compact access to an upper level. The crisp detailing and restrained palette, warm wood contrasting with sleek stainless steel, provide unity and cohesion.

TOP RIGHT An internal window provides borrowed light for a small bathroom. Small spaces can be dark: creating new openings is a good way of spreading available natural light. The pale décor and large mirror are also reflective.

BOTTOM LEFT A massive wooden column, part of the building's original structure, lends character to a converted loft. Elsewhere, detailing is kept to the minimum so there is little to distract the eye.

BOTTOM RIGHT These neatly detailed stairs allow light to spill through from the level above and do not block views. Bespoke stairs can also be commissioned from specialist outlets or designers.

PREVIOUS PAGES Furniture placement clearly defines different zones within a living/eating/cooking area. The half-width partition helps to screen kitchen activity.

ABOVE The removal of the wall that enclosed the staircase has created a much more expansive feeling in a basement kitchen. In an elegant detail, the mini breakfast bar reads as an extension of one of the stair treads.

OPPOSITE Floor-to-ceiling pivoting glass doors open up a small kitchen fully to the outdoors on fine days. Borrowed space, just as much as borrowed light, can go a long way to counteract any sense of confinement or enclosure.

OPENING UP

A key small space design strategy is to open up the interior as far as possible to enhance the quality of space. If you knock down a wall or two, you won't win much in the way of floor area per se, but the effect will be immediately expansive. The complexity (and expense) of the work will be determined by whether or not the wall or walls in question are load-bearing. A load-bearing wall plays an integral role in the structure of a building — remove it and you will have to put a compensatory element in its place, such as a steel joist. Partition walls, which are simply spatial dividers, can be taken down with impunity. If you are in any doubt about which walls are structural and which are not, consult a surveyor, engineer or architect.

Knocking two poky rooms together to create a single multipurpose space is one option. You may also wish to absorb a hallway into your main living space by removing the dividing wall. Similarly, removing the wall that

LEFT Areas that are double-height or where the ceilings are higher than standard lend themselves to vertical subdivision. Mezzanine or platform levels provide extra floor area for more private areas such as bedrooms or home offices without compromising the feeling of openness.

RIGHT In a clever and hard-working use of space, a compact kitchen has been slotted in beside the stairs. The U-shaped arrangement is one of the most workable of all kitchen layouts.

encloses a staircase can also open up the interior dramatically. But it is also important to remember to balance openness with a sense of enclosure. A fully open interior, where everything is out on view at all times, can be tiring and demanding to live in, providing no respite. Private space, where you can retreat for some peace and quiet when desired, is also essential.

VOLUME

Spatial quality is often a function of volume. Cutting away part of an upper level can help to draw light down from above and generate a feeling of uplift and drama that more than makes up for the loss of floor area. Similarly, stopping partitions short of the ceiling allows the full height of a space to be appreciated and allows light to filter through.

A few steps up or down – simple changes in level – can also add variety and richness to spatial experience. This strategy is a good way of signalling a change of activity – for example, a shift from a dining area to a living area.

SIMPLIFYING DETAIL

Successful small spaces play to their strengths. Often this entails stripping back and simplifying on the level of detail so there is not too much visual distraction. Restrained or minimal detailing keeps the focus where you want it.

Architectural detail such as skirting boards, mouldings and trim can look a little fussy in a small space, particularly when dividing walls have been removed, or when a property has been subdivided into a number of flats. Most period detailing only makes visual sense when rooms are proportioned accordingly in their original layout. If the detailing is of no great distinction, think about removing it altogether to crate cleaner lines.

BELOW LEFT A partition that is open on both sides separates a kitchen from a living area. Picked out in a warm, earthy shade, it makes a contrast with the all-white décor.

BELOW RIGHT Different activities are signalled by furniture arrangement. Long low lines mean that views are not obscured.

RIGHT A mezzanine level provides room for a home office bathed in natural light from roof windows.

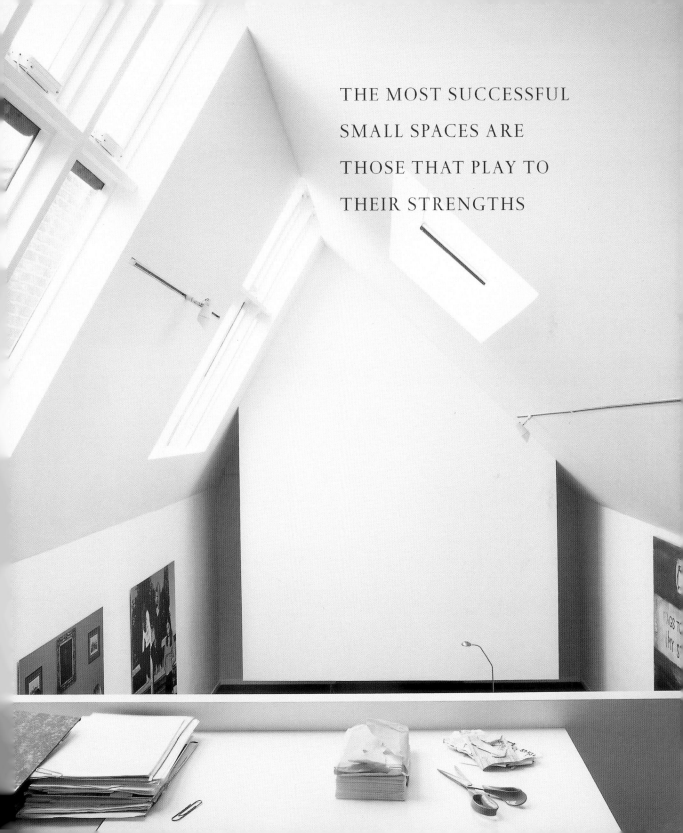

THE MOST SUCCESSFUL
SMALL SPACES ARE
THOSE THAT PLAY TO
THEIR STRENGTHS

LEFT An industrial staircase makes a bold insertion into the stripped-back house. These dogleg metal stairs take up less space than conventional types and allow light to spill down from above.

RIGHT Pleated plastic dividers provide flexible screening for a sleeping area on the upper level. A work area has been set up in the bay window at the far end, and benefits from additional top lighting from the glazed gable wall.

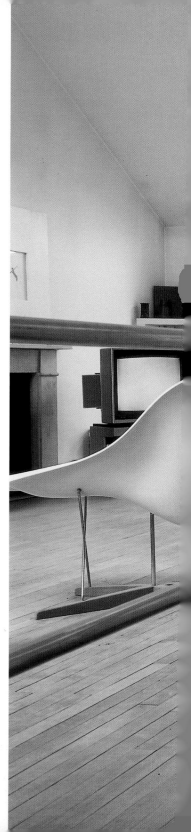

MODERN CONVERSION
AN EDWARDIAN SEMI-DETACHED HOUSE IN LONDON HAS BEEN OPENED UP TO CREATE FREE-FLOWING SPACES

Prior to its conversion, this house was a warren of small separate rooms. Faced with a similar layout, many people opt to take down a wall or two. The approach adopted here by architect J. F. Delsalle was far more radical and resulted in a complete reinvention of the interior. The house has been stripped back to its underlying structure and all period detailing removed.

On the ground floor, the ceiling was raised 50cm to give a greater sense of volume. This level now provides an inclusive living/eating/cooking area. A new industrial staircase connects to the level above, another open-plan space for working, sleeping and relaxing. To improve light the gable wall has been removed and the opening filled with glass. Skylights have been added.

The decorative approach is equally robust. Walls and ceilings are bare plaster. The flooring is lime-bleached oak. Against this muted backdrop, an eclectic blend of furnishings contribute character and personality – an Indian bed, an Eames chair, a Victorian settee and a reclaimed worktable.

THIS PAGE A secure metal ladder raked at an angle provides access to an upper level without taking up too much floor space.

Space-saving stairs

- Spiral stairs are an excellent space-saving solution and come in a wide variety of styles, from period pieces to contemporary designs.

- Paddle or monks' stairs, canted or vertical, have offset treads, which makes them narrower than conventional stairs.

- You can buy stairs off the peg or commission a custom design. Make sure the floor can bear the weight.

Stairs, hallways and landings can take up a disproportionate amount of space, particularly in older properties. In some circumstances, a standard staircase can be removed and a space-saving design substituted. Space-saving stairs are also a good way of providing access to a converted loft or mezzanine without sacrificing too much of the floor area on the level below.

There are many different types of compact staircases on the market; custom designs unique to your situation are another possibility. In all cases, the stairs must be robust enough for the use to which they will be subjected and conform to other regulations regarding pitch, the provision of handrails and so on.

ABOVE Curved or spiral stairs have inherent drama and theatricality.

RIGHT Stairs at their most minimal: steel rungs fixed to the wall. This arrangement is best used when the stairs are not in daily use.

FLEXIBLE LAYOUTS

LEFT Sliding Japanese
paper screens, or shoji,
are an elegant way of
partitioning space. The
paper is translucent,
which allows light through,
and the wood-framed
screens move readily at
the touch of a finger.

OPPOSITE Movable
partitions help you to keep
your spatial options open.
One way of enhancing
space is to extend sliding
doors or panels from
the floor right up to the
ceiling, so that when they
are open the space reads
seamlessly. The free-
standing shelving unit
serves as another form
of spatial divider.

Adaptability is increasingly what all of us require from
our homes these days. If you live in a small space, you will inevitably have to
think about ways in which different activities can be accommodated within the
same area. The social pursuits of cooking, eating and relaxing naturally group
well together, as do the private activities of sleeping and bathing.

In many successful small spaces, flexibility is literally built into the fabric.
Seamless walls of storage, concealed behind flush doors on press catches keep
everyday clutter under control and out of sight. A step further and you might
consider treating the working parts of your home – the kitchen and home office,
for example – in the same way, with elements that pull down, pull out or fold
away. This will allow you to reduce visual clutter when you use the same area
for relaxing or entertaining. Either custom or off-the-peg solutions are possible,
but it is important to remember that if you are going to be reconfiguring your
space on a regular basis, the fitted elements must be fully integrated and work
properly or you will be setting yourself up for daily frustration.

LEFT In this small apartment, the gridded steel-framed partitioning provides architectural character as well as flexibility. Along one side of the kitchen, the partition is mirrored, while the pivoting partitions that screen the sleeping area from the rest of the space are fitted with obscured textured glass for greater privacy.

RIGHT A lightweight concertina-folding fabric screen that slides along a metal track provides instant partitioning for a sleeping area.

Bear in mind that existing services, particularly water and drainage, are expensive to change and their location will probably dictate the siting of kitchen areas and bathrooms and the elements within them, for example. Less intrusive and expensive is making alterations to electrical provision. The more power points there are in a space, the more flexible it will be. You can also think about installing sockets in the floor, which will maximize potential for furniture arrangement and lighting. In a multipurpose area that includes a kitchen, make sure there is efficient mechanical extraction.

PARTITIONING

Partitions are a great way of keeping your options open and signalling the distinction between different areas of activity. They may be fixed – in the form of half-height counters or half-width portions of wall – or movable, such as sliding doors and free-standing screens. Doors that extend right up to the ceiling enhance the sense of space because they do not interrupt the planes of the floor and ceiling and allow adjoining areas to read as a continuous whole.

A counter that doubles up as a breakfast bar is a tried and tested way of screening a kitchen area in a multipurpose space, providing enclosure to conceal food preparation while retaining a general sense of openness. The same strategy can be adopted in a bedroom to separate a bathroom or dressing area, using a portion of wall like an over-scaled bedhead as a divider.

LEFT The two living areas are divided by a central steel staircase – an acid green glass panel serves as a baluster and provides a vivid colour accent. The bedroom is located on a mezzanine above this room.

RIGHT Blinds screen the window and glazed front door in the main living area to provide privacy. Although the floor area is very limited, dramatic top lighting from the glass roof makes the apartment seem much more spacious that it actually is.

SMALL IS BEAUTIFUL

ELEGANT DETAILING AND CLEVER DESIGN MAKES THE MOST OF LIMITED SPACE IN A PARISIAN PIED-A-TERRE

The small Parisian apartment designed by Gérard Faivre is located in a lean-to addition accessed directly from a courtyard. The space has been cleverly designed and decorated to dispel any hint of confinement. In the centre of the apartment, a steep steel staircase, with glass balusters tinted acid green rises up to a mezzanine level where the bedroom is situated. On the ground floor, the stairs separate two living areas, one of which is top lit by a glass roof. Down a short flight of steps is the kitchen and bathroom.

A key aspect of the success of the scheme is the subtle, sophisticated decoration. The main living area is decorated in three shades of grey, while the white-upholstered furniture is framed in steel. A Bordeaux rug adds texture, warmth and a touch of colour underfoot. The long low lines of the furniture are echoed in the low shelving built across the width of the space, which provides a place to prop pictures and display decorative objects.

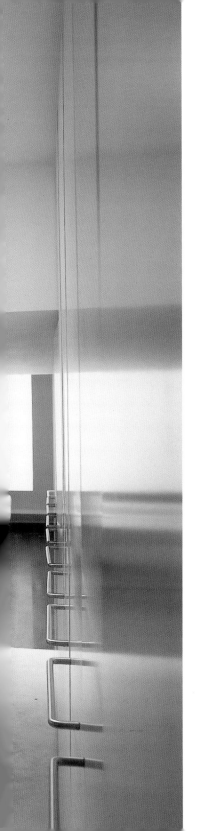

NATURAL LIGHT

The better the quality of natural light there is available, the more spacious your home will seem. If existing conditions are less than ideal, you can improve them in one of three ways: either by directly increasing the amount of daylight an area receives, by borrowing light from adjoining brighter areas, or by enhancing what light there is.

Adding a new window or enlarging an existing one can make all the difference if a particular area in your home is poorly lit. In many cases, this is structural work. You will need to install a beam or lintel over a new window or an existing window that has been widened to support the wall above. Think about siting – ideally you want to install the new window where you won't be overlooked and on a west- or south-facing aspect.

Daylight that comes from above is a feel-good factor of the first order and a natural way of enhancing space. Types of top lighting include skylights,

LEFT Light that comes from above is naturally space-enhancing and uplifting. This large circular skylight brings daylight into what would otherwise be a dark hallway.

RIGHT Part of the appeal of converted attics and lofts is the opportunity they offer for toplighting. There are many different designs of rooflight on the market, some of which are fixed and some of which are openable. Other types pivot for ease of cleaning.

BELOW Café curtains, hung from rods positioned midway up a window, provide privacy while allowing light to spill in above. Blinds are another good solution, and have the bonus of filtering light in interesting ways.

OPPOSITE Pure white décor creates a tranquil, ethereal mood and makes the most of natural light. Here great care has been taken to ensure that different surfaces and materials are all in the same tone of white, which can be tricky to get right.

rooflights, glazed roofs and high-level or clerestory windows. For maximum effect, site top lighting over stairs or landings so that the light introduced can spill down through several levels, over a working area such as a kitchen counter where good natural lighting is essential, or over a bed or bath where you can appreciate the changing light levels.

BORROWING LIGHT

Making what natural light is available go further can be accomplished in a wide variety of ways. These include:

- Creating new internal openings. Internal windows not only spread the light around, they set up views and vistas that banish any hint of confinement. Portholes, squares, vertical or horizontal strips – new openings can be any shape or size.
- Removing unnecessary partitions and opening up stairs.
- Using glazing internally for doors and partitions.
- Installing glass walkways at upper levels.
- Reallocating space. Think about siting living areas on upper floors where the quality of light is better, and bedrooms down below.

ENHANCING LIGHT

The classic way of enhancing natural light is through sympathetic decoration. Light toned surfaces and finishes are reflective and fresh looking. Glass, metal and other glossy materials also catch the light and generate a sense of vitality. Judiciously placed mirrors – opposite a window or doorway – spread available light around.

How you dress your windows will also have an impact on the quality of light. Curtains that can be fully opened or blinds that can be raised up, exposing the entire surface of the glazed area, admit maximum light into the interior. If you require privacy during the day, but don't want to block light, one solution is to use blinds that pull up from the base of the window, leaving the topmost portion uncovered. Slatted blinds and other louvred treatments offer flexibility and can filter the light in evocative ways, throwing interesting shadows; stained glass tints the light with glowing colour.

THE CLASSIC WAY OF
ENHANCING NATURAL LIGHT
IS THROUGH THE USE OF
SYMPATHETIC DECORATION

LEFT A glazed end wall leads onto a narrow decked terrace with a view over a small city garden. An eating area can be fairly circumscribed yet not feel claustrophobic when there's a view to appreciate. The use of timber flooring inside and out underscores the connection.

RIGHT Getting away from it all: a snug A-frame cabin makes the perfect weekend retreat. The bed, with its Hudson Bay blanket, looks out over the surrounding countryside.

OUTSIDE IN

These days we all enjoy spaces that offer easy connection with the world outside. If your home is small, blurring the boundaries between outside and in will have a huge impact on spatial quality. You don't need a great deal of room – balconies or roof terraces offer potential. Take advantage of any opportunity to connect with outdoor areas wherever you find it.

Blend internal and external areas by creating new openings or enlarging existing ones and infilling them with glass. You may wish to replace a single door that gives access to a garden or terrace with French windows – or go even further and glaze an end wall. Floor-to-ceiling sliding or folding glazed doors that can be fully opened on fine days turn outdoor areas into a direct extension of your living space. This is also true at upper levels where the 'garden' may be limited to a small balcony or roof terrace.

When space is really tight, extending your home may be the only practical way of improving matters. Glazed extensions offer the best of both worlds – you gain the extra floor area you require and what you sacrifice in terms of garden or external areas is compensated by bringing the outside world closer

LEFT AND BELOW The side return is a popular site for increasing the floor area of a terraced or semi-detached house. In this case, every attempt has been made to integrate the new kitchen with the garden. A sloping glass roof bathes the space in natural light. The same flooring unites inside and outside, and a stone counter links them so that they read as one space.

OPPOSITE Even a small amount of outdoor space can be hugely beneficial. This decked balcony-cum-terrace provides a place for outdoor eating and somewhere to grow a bit of greenery.

to home. Many older terraced properties, for example, have narrow and more or less redundant strips of land along the side return, which often provide ideal sites for extensions. Glazing the roof of a side-return extension can also transform the quality of light in adjacent areas.

When you are using glass on this scale, it's important to specify the right type. Extensive glazing can mean excessive heat loss in winter and overheating in summer. Other practical issues include cleaning, maintenance and safety. High-specification glass can be expensive, but it is often worth the investment. Types include low-emissivity glass that reflects heat back into the interior; self-cleaning glass, which has a special coating that destroys organic dirt, ideal for hard-to-reach high-level windows; and shatterproof safety glass.

Reinforce the sense of connection by matching materials tonally and texturally — a hardwood floor that leads out to a decked area, for example, or stone indoors and out. You can also render and paint a boundary wall so that it reads as the furthest extent of the interior. Another visual trick is to extend a kitchen counter into the outdoor space so that it creates an unbroken line.

THIS PAGE A platform that provides room for a raised living room doubles up as integrated concealed storage space serving the kitchen and eating area.

Mezzanine levels

- Think about siting carefully: you don't want to block views and light.

- Access is important: spiral stairs or paddle steps won't use too much floor area.

- If the platform is not huge, you can fit out the area below with built-in storage.

- A larger space below might be a good location for a kitchen and dining area.

In areas where ceilings are higher than standard subdividing space vertically can win you much-needed additional floor area. Double-height spaces offer the most potential, but even the ceiling height that is found in many older properties, for example, gives you something to play with. With this type of alteration the principal distinction is between a mezzanine level, which is a structural alteration because the load is carried by the existing walls, and a simple platform, which is self-supported in some way or built up from the floor.

Mezzanines and platforms offer a degree of separation from the main living area and are ideal for activities that require a greater degree of peace and quiet such as sleeping and working.

ABOVE Room at the top: a sleeping platform does not require full head height.

RIGHT A fully fledged mezzanine level differs from a simple platform in that the weight of the floor is generally carried by the existing walls.

RIGHT The main living room is double height. An internal window provides a view of the bathroom and its decorative mirror.

BELOW The bedroom on the mezzanine level is minimally furnished and decorated in white.

OPPOSITE One half of the apartment has been subdivided vertically, with a kitchen and eating area tucked under a mezzanine level, accessed by stairs to the rear. To the left, a passage lined with open larder shelves leads to an internal bathroom.

INTERNAL WINDOWS
A DOUBLE-HEIGHT SPACE IN A MODERN PARISIAN BLOCK FEATURES INTERNAL OPENINGS TO SPREAD LIGHT

Spaces that are double height provide great scope for vertical subdivision. The challenge is then to ensure that internal areas have natural light. This compact apartment, designed by Tristan Auer, is essentially a long tall box that has been divided in two. The main living space is double-height and bathed in light from large windows. The other half of the apartment has been fitted with a mezzanine level, where a bedroom and workspace are located. Underneath is a kitchen/eating area and an internal bathroom.

To enhance the sense of space and spread available light around, the spaces on the mezzanine level are screened with glass panels. Below, another internal window lights the bathroom and provides views through to the living area. This transparency also adds clarity to the design. One wall of the kitchen is lined with bookshelves that continue on the level above. Thanks to the openness, the wall reads as one unbroken plane.

OPPOSITE A photomural adds to the charm of a small cloakroom concealed within a built-in storage wall. The flush doors are on press-catches for a seamless effect.

LEFT Tucked beneath the stairs is a built-in seating area, making the most of what would otherwise be redundant space.

BELOW Hidden spaces have great psychological appeal. Who can resist the temptation to curl up on a window seat with a good book or simply watch the world go by?

HIDDEN SPACES

When your home is small, every bit of it has to work for its keep. That means putting otherwise redundant areas to some use. In many homes, the space under the stairs, if it is used at all, often ends up as some kind of glory hole, stashed with odds and ends that don't really have a proper home. Fitted out properly, however, it could provide an additional seating area, a home office, a utility cupboard or some other type of dedicated storage area. Stairs, too, offer potential. Stair treads can be transformed into drawers or stowing places for a range of different items. Once this meant a custom solution but there are now companies offering ready-made stairs fitted with storage compartments.

Generous landings are the ideal site for free-standing or fitted storage. A handsome chest or armoire can serve as a place to keep linen or you can build in

LEFT Converting an attic or a loft is a great way of gaining extra space. These quirky, angled spaces are ideal for bedrooms or studies, being out of the way of the rest of the household. This attic retreat is warmed by the flue of a solid fuel stove.

RIGHT The exposed beams and trusses in this attic bedroom provide a natural distinction between a sleeping area and the bathtub.

a wall of sleek unobtrusive drawers and cupboards. If there is enough floor area, you could also set up a home office on a landing. Loft conversions are deservedly one of the most popular of all home alterations and there are many specialist companies who will design the space for you, obtain the necessary permissions if required and carry out the work. Any loft that has adequate head height can be transformed into another room or rooms. It used to be the case that certain types of roof structure ruled out conversion, but nowadays this is no longer the case. Even if your loft or attic space is not big enough to be converted to a room, a minimum amount of fitting out will turn it into valuable storage space.

Does your car really need to be under cover? If you have a garage, particularly one that is built on to the house, it can be absorbed into your home with a minimum of expense and disruption by extending services into the space, laying new surfaces and finishes and perhaps creating a new connecting door if one does not already exist.

Although undoubtedly expensive and disruptive, converting basements or enlarging existing ones is becoming an increasingly popular way of gaining more space. This is largely due to improved damp-proofing techniques that redirect ground water. Getting natural light down into the new area can be a challenge: pavement lights, lightwells and atria are typical solutions.

STORAGE

When it comes to making small spaces truly liveable and workable, providing adequate storage is at least half the battle. It's a two-pronged attack to make it work. On the one hand, you have to cast a critical and rigorous eye over your belongings and only offer house-room to what is necessary or desirable. On the other, you have to think about systems of organization that support everyday activities efficiently, so that you can find what you want the instant you need it.

We're all familiar with the concept of the capsule wardrobe – those essential items of clothing that work well together whatever the occasion. When you live in a small space, it's a good idea to apply the same principle to other categories of possessions, from kitchen equipment to tableware. For example, you don't need different sets of crockery for everyday and best: one good all-purpose set will do. In the same way, you won't need separate

ABOVE LEFT Successful small space living demands careful storage. Built-in cupboards can house a vast amount of everyday clutter without impinging on available space.

ABOVE RIGHT A wall-mounted rack and wooden hangers makes a space-saving alternative to the standard hall coat-stand.

RIGHT A whole-hearted approach to storage better than a series of individual or piecemeal solutions. Here an entire wall has been fitted with book shelves and the effect is coherent not cluttered.

serving dishes if your ovenware is handsome enough to put straight on the table. Weeding out what is surplus to requirements can mean facing a few home truths. But bear in mind that clutter tends to accumulate however disciplined you are and that you will need to undertake similar reviews on a fairly regular basis. Here are some ideas for lightening the load:

- Get rid of anything that is making you feel guilty: clothes that don't fit or that don't suit you, books you will never read, things that you have been given that you don't like; any equipment or kit related to an activity you no longer pursue; things that have been awaiting repair for ages.
- Keep abreast of paperwork and file or dispose of anything that does not relate to current household matters, including old manuals, out of date service bills and so on.
- Extend the same critical approach to new acquisitions. Before you commit yourself to buying ask yourself, first do you need it, second do you like it and third where are you going to put it?

OPPOSITE Storage does not mean that everything has to be hidden from view; working areas such as kitchens lend themselves to a certain amount of display. Here, open shelves serve as a larder for foodstuffs, all neatly decanted into storage jars.

BELOW LEFT An array of glassware is displayed on shelves cantilevered from the wall. The vibrant blue gives added impact.

BELOW RIGHT Robust professional-style metal shelving provides a place to store pots and pans in everyday use.

LEFT Concealed storage behind raised blank panels has an almost sculptural presence. When you are building in storage space, it is essential to tailor the dimensions to the size of items you are intending to keep there.

THIS PAGE A wall dividing an en suite bathroom from a sleeping area has been fitted out on one side with drawers for clothes storage. The recess above is mirrored and is lit by downlights.

GETTING ORGANIZED

Storage solutions broadly fall into two distinct categories: fitted and unfitted. It's fair to say that fitted storage works best in small spaces, particularly in areas that feature fixed elements themselves, such as kitchens and bathrooms. The effect is less obtrusive and you are able to exploit every last millimetre of space. However, when it comes to fitted storage, one size doesn't fit all. You may need to customize the interior of units, cupboards and closets to make the most of them. Here are a few ideas:

■ Adjustable shelving to accommodate possessions of different heights.
■ Narrow shelving for small items.
■ Drawer dividers for storing cutlery and kitchen utensils or for separating small accessories.
■ Boxes and baskets for grouping like with like.
■ Racks and rails fitted to the backs of cupboard doors.

THIS PAGE A slim-line radiator mounted vertically on the wall is an attractive feature in its own right.

Space-saving heating

- If you can't afford a complete overhaul of your central heating system, invest in space-saving radiators.

- Compact low-level radiators hug the base of the wall.

- Dramatic sculptural shapes like coils can be mounted vertically or horizontally.

- Ladder-like radiators that double up as heated towel rails are ideal for bathrooms.

Most of the servicing that forms the infrastructure to your home – electricity, water, drainage, gas supply – is routed within the fabric of walls, ceilings or floors and does not take up usable space. The same is not always true of heating. Central heating radiators may well be intrusive both because of their design and their position, limiting your options for furniture arrangement and built-in storage.

The most space-saving type of heating is under-floor. There are various types but the most common consists of elements built into the structure under the final flooring. It is most effective used with a flooring material that has high thermal mass, such as stone, tile or concrete – materials that warm up slowly and retain heat for longer.

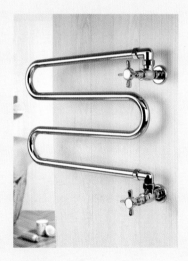

ABOVE Heated towel rails combine storage for linen with ambient space heating, ideal for small bathrooms.

RIGHT Radiators that hug the base of the wall are much less obtrusive.

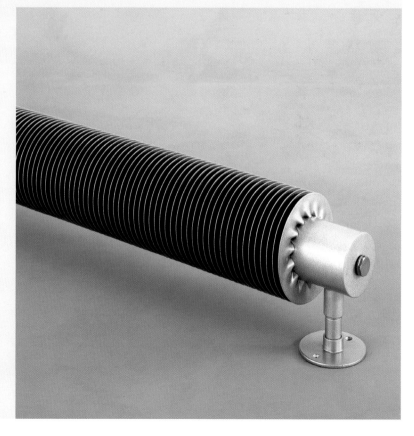

Style

Many of the tried and tested strategies for small-space living – simplified detailing, discreet fitted storage, and a general absence of clutter of any description – are designed to maximize the efficiency of your home and make the most of every available square foot. But homes are more than 'machines for living': they play a central psychological role. When you walk through the door, your home should feel it is yours, otherwise you might as well be living in a hotel.

Style is a key way of expressing our own personal tastes. When your home is compact, getting the basic framework right is vitally important. But it doesn't stop there. How you decorate – the colours, materials and patterns you choose – is what brings enjoyment and a real sense of belonging into the equation. It is what makes the difference between a home that is bland and banal and one that remains a source of delight.

Decorating rooms that are restricted in size and proportion needs a careful hand and a certain degree of planning. Before you take the plunge, assemble swatches of fabric, samples of materials and pots of paint and play around with different combinations. Then go with your instinct. Allow yourself to enjoy your favourite colour or a pattern you find irresistible. Display is important. Banishing clutter is well and good, but make sure you find the room for a few of your favourite things, those objects and pictures that have meaning for you.

TOP LEFT A shiny black tablecloth provides graphic contrast to white décor. Keeping it simple is always a good idea in a small space, but that need not entail blandness.

TOP RIGHT Patterned surfaces and finishes, as long as they are not too dominant, can introduce a welcome note of rhythm and vitality.

BELOW LEFT Doors and the panels of concealed storage are decorated in off-white - just enough of a difference set against the crisp white walls to bring out their sculptural quality.

BELOW RIGHT White décor makes the most of natural light and reduces the visual bulk of furniture. This scheme is grounded by the wooden floor and fire surround.

PREVIOUS PAGES A subtle palette of colours and a confident mix of materials strikes a note of understated chic in a kitchen and eating area. The pebble mosaic tiling gives textural depth. Pale green unit fronts make a sympathetic foil to the warmth of the wooden surfaces.

WHITE ON WHITE

Airy, luminous and reflective, white is classic small-space décor. Elegant in some settings, fresh and unassuming in others, white always makes the most of light and enhances the sense of space. As it has no obvious stylistic overtones – or so many – it works just as well with traditional furnishings and detailing as it does in clean-lined contemporary rooms.

Don't be fooled into thinking that white equals absence of colour. White is a colour and a very subtle one, or perhaps it is truer to say that it is a family of tones. Ivory, cream, chalk and pearl are not simply seductive names dreamt up by paint manufacturers to tempt us, they describe elusive but very real differences between whiter shades of pale.

The big divide is between cool whites and warm whites. Cool whites have a touch of pigment from the cool end of the spectrum – blue, grey or black. Warm whites contain hints of warm earthier colours. Which white you choose for a particular area depends on the quality of natural light. Cool white in a north- or east-facing room will be dreary and dispiriting: it belongs in sunnier rooms with south- or west-facing aspects, where it will be fresh and invigorating. Warm white softens cool north light and makes it cosy and hospitable.

LEFT White decoration has the effect of suppressing detail, which helps to enhance the sense of space. It can be every bit as dramatic as the most vivid colour, creating an other-worldly effect.

RIGHT It's important to choose the right white for the setting. Warm whites suit north-facing locations or those that do not benefit from a good quality of natural light.

WHITE DOES NOT EQUAL

ABSENCE OF COLOUR – IT

IS ITSELF A COLOUR

ALBEIT A SUBTLE ONE

THIS PAGE Different whites can look awkward in combination. What makes the creamy off-white upholstery work with the pure white coffee table and painted floorboards are the touches of yellow.

Be prepared to spend some time choosing the right white and paying decent money for it. Cheap white paints, especially the ones marketed as 'brilliant', should be left on the shelf. They lack the depth of true cool whites and are simply glaring. The ubiquitous 'magnolia' is insipid rather than warm. Good quality white paint is much more sophisticated and will also mellow sympathetically over the course of time.

White is widely assumed to be a fail-safe option, quiet and unassuming. While it's true that white is inherently restful, in large doses it can be remarkably dramatic, making a powerful statement in its own right. White walls, white floors and white furnishings, used in combination, create an ethereal, almost other-worldly setting.

In small spaces, white on a grand scale brings many benefits. Most importantly it minimizes the bulk of large pieces of furniture such as sofas and beds. As a reticent background, it throws the focus onto form and shape, uniting different surfaces and suppressing detail.

To keep white rooms alive and full of vitality, ring the changes with different textures and finishes, from matt through to high gloss. You can also combine different whites for an elegant layering of tones and add a dash of accent colour or the graphic contrast of black.

RIGHT A restricted palette means you can include more detailing in a small area without running the risk of undermining the sense of space with clutter. Here the mellow brick floor provides the only hint of colour.

LEFT The exposed chimney breast, with its stepped sides, provides a natural separation. At the far end of the apartment an entire wall has been lined with shelves to store a library accessed by a white ladder.

BELOW A pair of bunk beds have been built into a wall next to the chimney breast. The paint used throughout has a soft matt texture.

RIGHT The kitchen is located against the other end wall. Natural light floods down from the rooflights slotted into the plane of the roof above.

SWEDISH STYLE
AN APARTMENT IN STOCKHOLM HAS BEEN TRANSFORMED INTO AN AIRY, LUMINOUS EXPRESSION OF SWEDISH STYLE

White is a great unifier, as this attic demonstrates. The former owners had subdivided the top floor space and covered up the existing structure as far as possible. Designer Martine Colliander adopted the opposite approach, exposing beams, chimney stack and original brick flooring and removing walls to create an open-plan layout and to reveal the unique character. The result could have looked cluttered, but all-white décor and furnishings serve to create a harmonious whole. The structural details, such as the beams and stepped sides of the chimney stack, are still evident, but they do not dominate. The only colour is the muted tones of the brick flooring.

In Scandinavian décor, both traditional and modern, white is always a positive choice, not a fail-safe option. So, while the furniture in this apartment is chiefly traditional in design, the liberal use of white prevents the overall effect from looking too self-consciously period.

MATERIAL QUALITY

One great advantage of small-space living is that because surface areas are limited, you can afford better quality materials. Tiling a small bathroom in natural stone is an affordable luxury; double the size of the space and you're looking at a second mortgage.

Decorating with materials in mind brings depth and character into play. It means thinking about texture, the way different surfaces sound and feel, how they age and wear. By and large, it is natural materials – stone, wood, terracotta and textiles made from natural fibres – that have the most soul. Synthetics are generally cheaper – if you don't count the environmental cost of producing them – but they degrade over time. A worn stone floor is charming. A worn vinyl floor is shabby. Paint is a quick cover-up and a relatively inexpensive one. If you make a mistake and choose the wrong shade, you can rectify it without too much heartbreak. Materials, on the

LEFT A shift in flooring material from painted concrete to hardwood defines a kitchen in an open-plan loft, with the table bridging the two sides of the divide. The table legs on the kitchen side have been shortened to allow for the difference in height between the two surfaces.

RIGHT Small space living means you can afford better materials because you will not be dealing with very large areas. Good detailing is crucial, especially in those areas where different materials abut each other.

other hand, require a greater degree of time and investment. Once the floor
is laid, the tiles are grouted or the counter is installed, it's a bit late in the
day to discover that the effect is not what you wanted.

Planning is essential. Before you commit to a purchase, it's a good idea to
assemble samples of different materials and live with them in your home to
assess what they look like under different light conditions.
Other points to consider:

■ How does the material perform? Is it suitable for the use to which it will be
put? For example, flooring in areas of heavy traffic needs to be robust.
Kitchen counters should be heat-proof and stain-proof. Bathroom surfaces
should be water-resistant and non-slip underfoot.

LEFT Wooden walls and
furniture painted the same
pale blue-grey unites the
interior with the exterior
and creates an informal
summery setting. A few
species of wood, such as
larch, cedar and teak, are
naturally weather-
resistant; otherwise, paints
and seals have to be
renewed regularly to
prevent deterioration.

RIGHT Panels faced in
hardwood veneer make a
striking architectural
statement in this
mezzanine sleeping area.
Strong contrasts of
material can be very
effective in small spaces.

- How is the material installed? Heavy materials require adequate support and professional installation. Some materials require special fixings or adhesives or particular types of underlay.
- What kind of maintenance is required? Does the material need to be sealed or dressed after installation? How easy is it to keep clean?

In a small space, you will need to choose one or two materials to act as unifying elements and one or two to serve as contrasts or focal points. Using the same tiles in the kitchen as in the bathroom, for example, or running the same flooring throughout your home, creates a subtle sense of connection. On the other hand, a contrasting material can signal a shift of activity without overt means of separation. A feature wall clad in veneered wood can define a dining area, in the same way a rug can anchor a seating arrangement.

LEFT Concrete has a reputation as a brutal material. Here, however, the cast in situ countertop, which extends to form bench seating, has a soft burnished finish to elevate it above the ordinary.

RIGHT A textured concrete partition screens a sleeping area and forms an unusual bedhead. The flooring displays the same mottled texture.

LEFT The kitchen blends steel appliances with redwood storage cupboards. The flooring is riven slate. Throughout the apartment, Japanese paper lanterns define different areas of activity.

BELOW The tatami room forms a private enclosure within what is essentially an open-plan space.

RIGHT The bathroom is separated from the corridor by shoji paper-covered screens. Chrome fittings and fixtures gleam against the blue-grey slate walls and floor. The corridor is bamboo-clad.

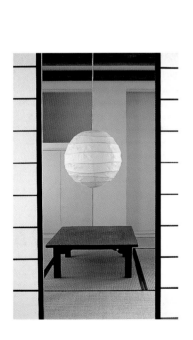

EASTERN INSPIRATION
A JAPANESE SENSIBILITY INFORMS THE DESIGN OF A LONDON APARTMENT, CREATING A SERENE CONTEMPLATIVE SPACE

Designed by architects Ushida Findlay, this loft apartment provides a contemporary take on Eastern living and incorporates certain key elements of traditional Japanese design. In traditional Japanese houses, the dimensions of the tatami mat, a cushioned floor covering made of straw, serves as a module for spatial design, with different interior spaces sized according to the number of mats that fit into them. Typically, interior spaces are also flexibly divided by shoji, paper-covered screens.

The spine of the layout is a corridor that runs from the sitting area at the front of the apartment to the private sleeping and bathing areas at the rear. Midway along is the kitchen and the tatami room, which serves as a guest room. The entire corridor is lined in bamboo, behind which is concealed storage space for clothes, books and everyday necessities.

LEFT It takes a certain degree of confidence, but small spaces can take big statements, whether that comes in the form of strong colour, pattern or a distinctive period theme.

RIGHT Chocolate brown walls, elegantly contrasted with white woodwork and detailing, make an atmospheric backdrop for a small dining room, reinforcing a sense of intimacy and enclosure.

MAKING A STATEMENT

You don't have to say goodbye to your sense of personal style just because your home is on the small side. Pale and interesting is not the only way to go. Small spaces can readily accommodate big statements if you keep to a few simple rules. As ever, it is crucial to think about your home as a whole. If you are drawn to a particular style or period of decorating, extend the whole theme throughout. In a small space you don't have the luxury of ringing the changes from room to room or area to area: that would be indigestible. Colour is an incredibly energizing element and has a powerful impact on atmosphere and mood. Forget about wishy-washy pastels and treat yourself to those shades that sing out to you.

The simplest way of using strong colour in a small space is as an accent. This can be as incidental as the colours decorative objects or soft furnishings bring to the picture or as bold as a brightly painted feature wall.

LEFT Aside from the olive green wall behind the bed, most of the touches of colour here derive from soft furnishings, objects and details – elements that can be easily changed.

RIGHT Liberal doses of blue, grey and turquoise in this Moorish-inspired interior create a soothing tranquil mood. Colours from the cool end of the spectrum are said to be 'distancing' and hence more space-enhancing.

BELOW One of the simplest ways to inject strong colour in a restricted space is to confine it to a single feature wall and allow it plenty of breathing space.

Another strategy is to contain the colour so that your entire home is not dominated by it. Good places for bold colour statements are self-contained areas like bathrooms or enclosed hallways and stairs where the colour acts as a vibrant thread connecting other areas, but you don't run the risk of being overwhelmed by it. But beware of the foreshortening effects of certain colours: warm colours are 'advancing' and draw the eye.

The most challenging approach of all is to assemble a palette of three or four shades that work well together, at least one of which should be a vivid accent – you can take as your starting point a favourite painting, rug or decorative period, and work out from that. This palette should then form the basis of your entire decorative scheme. Even when colours are strong, there is no risk of visual muddle if they are repeated throughout your home so that everything ties together.

PATTERN AND SCALE

Today's bold prints, with their large over-scaled repeats, paradoxically suit small spaces very well. The effect is to defy the limitations of space rather than treat these as a drawback to be remedied. Small-scale patterns, on the other hand, are rarely successful and can be rather smothering.

Bold patterns with large-scale motifs are best used as accents. You don't have to paper a whole room with a particular design or upholster your sofa and chairs in the same patterned fabric. Make a statement with a feature wall or one stand-out piece of furniture and allow plenty of breathing space around it so that you can appreciate the effect.

LEFT Pattern at its most muted: a simple striped wallpaper lends architectural character to a bedroom tastefully decorated in neutral tones.

RIGHT Decorative displays have a pattern of their own. The rhythm of the spines on the bookshelves contribute as much to the vitality of this living room as the patterned cushions and decorative rug.

RIGHT The counter and cabinets are curved to accommodate the awkward angles of the space. Curves are more expensive to execute than straight lines, but can be highly effective.

LEFT The vivid green of the counter, repeated on the breakfast bar, draws attention to the curved design and away from angles and corners. Lilac, chosen for the walls, is a strong partner. It is also from the cool end of the spectrum and keeps the effect airy and expansive.

COLOUR AND PROPORTION
VIBRANT COLOUR IN A NORTH LONDON KITCHEN
ACCENTUATES AN UNUSUAL CURVED AND FLUID LAYOUT

Small spaces that are not regularly shaped pose an additional challenge. This kitchen forms part of what was previously a much higher room, as can be seen by the way the ceiling, which has been lowered, cuts away around the window. With angles to accommodate, a conventional rectilinear arrangement might well have been unworkable. Instead the solution was to create a curve, which unifies the space and irons out visual anomalies.

Here colour plays a key role in the success of the scheme. The choice of glossy bright green for the counter top draws the eye to the curve and minimizes the angles of the walls. The same colour, and curve, is picked up on the circular breakfast bar. The walls are in a vibrant shade of lilac, a cool distancing colour, while a decorative diamond pattern in red, green, lilac and yellow provides a vivid accent and includes the two dominant colours.

Room by Room

Many small space strategies

work across the board. Others are more specific and relate to particular types of activity and the areas in which they are most likely to be carried out. What works in a living room, for example, where the emphasis is on relaxation and comfort, won't necessarily work in an essentially functional space such as a kitchen. This section takes a look at each area in the home and suggests ways to furnish, light and equip them to make the most of whatever space you have available.

Before moving onto specifics, however, it is worth thinking about room allocation overall. You don't have to be living in a shoebox to be feeling the pinch in some aspects of your domestic life. Sometimes the solution is to take a long hard look at how you have apportioned space and consider whether it might make sense to swap things around. When children are small, for example, and can still share a room, it often makes sense to give them the biggest bedroom where they can spread out their toys and play, easing pressure on other areas. In the same way, if you're working from home most of the time, you might want to forego a separate dining room in favour of a home office, and set up an eating area in the kitchen or living room. And don't neglect the potential of hallways and between-spaces, which can often be fitted out with cupboards and shelves to decant clutter from adjoining areas.

TOP LEFT Where space is tight over all, it makes good sense to combine kitchens with eating areas, since the two activities are naturally related. A built-in bench, the continuation of a counter, separates the two spaces.

TOP RIGHT Devoting an entire wall to shelving, including the portion above the door, is a whole-hearted approach to storage that works well in a small space.

BELOW LEFT Today's small-scale wall-mounted bathroom fixtures and fittings allow you to fit out the tiniest cloakroom without sacrificing practicality.

BELOW RIGHT Clever storage pays dividends in space gained. The area under this day bed serves as a place to keep logs for the stove.

PREVIOUS PAGES Converted attics, where the headroom can be circumscribed, make good locations for sleeping areas. This bedhead built in under the eaves provides a shelf for a display of objects.

LIVING AREAS

When your home is on the small side, the living room will
inevitably play multiple roles. Perhaps you use it as a place to eat or work;
perhaps it forms part of an open-plan space that includes a kitchen. But
whatever extra functions you expect it to fulfil, it must serve first and
foremost as a place to relax and unwind from the stresses of everyday life. To
achieve this, you may well need to provide an element of separation between
different activities – screens or transparent partitions that allow you to put
some psychological distance between, for example, the sofa and your desk.

Sensitive lighting can make all the difference between a living room that
is welcoming and comfortable and one that is not. If your living area serves
more than one function, it is essential to control lighting with a dimmer
switch so you can vary light levels accordingly. Any space that is uniformly lit
automatically seems more confining. Overhead or central lights are best

ABOVE LEFT Living areas
these days often play more
than one role. To support
different activities,
adequate storage is
necessary. Books,
magazines, DVDs and CDs
are all easily shelved.

RIGHT The very least your
living room should provide
is a place for relaxation.
Here an upholstered bench
doubles as a table and
extra seating.

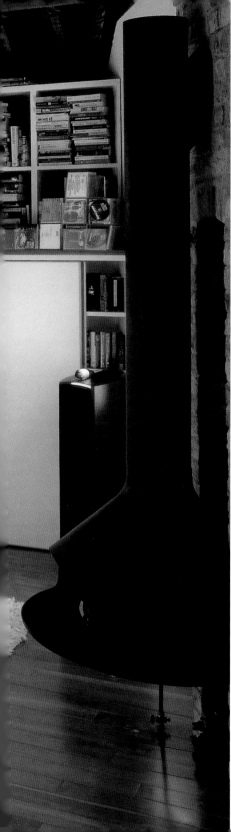

LEFT Built into the fabric of the room, this working wall of storage combines concealed shelving for organizing media players with open cubbyholes above. Flat screen TVs are easily concealed behind sliding panels, so your living room does not have to be dominated by electronic equipment.

RIGHT An eating area within a living room is tucked into a corner and defined by a framed collection of photographs.

avoided for that reason. They can also cause glare, which is tiring, and will cast shadows in the corners, which will make the walls appear to draw in. In living areas fixed downlights tend to emphasize the bulk of sofas and other seat furniture and create a rather static atmosphere.

Instead, vary the angle and position of lights to provide a sense of comfort and vitality. Strategically placed lamps create pools of light and shade that lead the eye. Uplighters bouncing off the ceiling enhance the sense of volume. Spots, which wash the walls with light, make a room seem more spacious.

STORAGE

Relaxation is incompatible with clutter. Unfortunately, many of the ways we choose to relax – watching TV, listening to music, playing on the computer – bring clutter in their wake. It's not just the visual intrusion of electronic gadgetry, it's the videos, DVDs and CDs that go with them. Wherever possible opt for concealed storage to provide necessary breathing space. Take advantage of advances in technology and invest in media equipment that comes in smaller, thinner forms – flatscreen TVs, for example, can be neatly hidden behind sliding panels; miniature speakers still deliver rich sound.

FURNITURE

Many people respond to the challenge of furnishing a small living area by opting for compact seating. All too often, this points up the limitation of the space without delivering real comfort. A better solution is to restrict the number of incidental chairs and tables and go for a couple of decent-sized sofas or some form of modular seating. If your living room is where you put up overnight guests, you may wish to invest in a sofa bed. Don't be tempted to skimp on quality. Cheap sofa beds are uncomfortable to sit and sleep on.

You can minimize the impact of large pieces of furniture in a number of ways. White, pale or neutral upholstery reduces visual bulk. Furniture that has long low lines is less dominant because views are not interrupted by high backs or sides. See-through designs in glass, Perspex or wire mesh are also space-enhancing. Think about arrangement, too. Any area will seem larger if the floor is kept clear and routes are not cluttered by unnecessary obstacles.

ABOVE LEFT Living room furniture can be bulky, but the answer is not necessarily to downsize. Positioning large items against the wall, in alcoves or in corners helps to keep the floor area clear.

RIGHT Modular seating is ideally suited to small-space living. These two daybeds, arranged to turn a corner, provide generous but inconspicuous seating.

FURNITURE WITH

LONG LOW LINES

IS LESS DOMINANT

LEFT Simplicity is the best strategy when it comes to furnishing a small living room. Two sofas facing each other across a single low bench look much neater than a collection of small chairs and occasional tables scattered about the place.

KITCHENS

These days, kitchens have acquired other roles apart from the obvious. With the decline of the separate dining room, they are where many families sit down to meals. They also tend to serve as a cross between command post and an informal place to entertain friends. For all of these reasons, it often makes sense to open up layouts so that the kitchen becomes part of a more inclusive cooking/eating/living space.

If that isn't possible, and you have to squeeze a kitchen into a tight space, don't despair. There's no reason why good cooking can't come out of small kitchens. Many serious cooks, amateur as well as professional, operate in quite restricted areas. Some prefer it that way. Restaurant kitchens are generally laid out so that maximum floor area can be devoted to tables full of customers. But small well-planned kitchens have their own appeal – it's about being in control and having everything within reach of your fingertips.

The key is good planning. Most successful small kitchens are fully fitted. Free-standing kitchen furniture takes up too much floor area and looks messier. Layout will be determined by the shape of the space you have available and where existing services are laid on – rearranging drainage and gas supply is disrupting and expensive.

One efficient compact layout is the galley kitchen, where units and appliances are built in on facing walls. A layout where everything is arranged in a single line is easy to screen behind sliding doors or panels. An L-shaped layout is a good way of incorporating a small kitchen area into an all-purpose living area. The projecting peninsula can screen preparation areas and double up as a counter to eat at.

When planning a small hard-working area such as a kitchen, dimensions are critical. Slotting it all in is one thing, but you need to make sure the space is workable in practice, that there is enough room to open oven, dishwasher and fridge doors, for example, and that you have enough elbow room for one or maybe two people. The longest stretch of worktop should be between the sink and hob, where most food preparation takes place.

LEFT A glazed end wall bathes the kitchen in natural light, providing ideal conditions for work that involves attention to detail. The absence of wall units gives the space a stream-lined look. In-line layouts, where the kitchen is arranged along the length of a wall, are very workable provided there is not too great a distance between the hob, sink and fridge.

STORAGE

With careful planning, there is no reason why a small kitchen cannot be an efficient and hard-working area. But kitchens are not simply about preparing and cooking food, they must also serve as storage areas for a whole range of different things, in different shapes and sizes – from cutlery and glassware to kitchen utensils and foodstuffs. When your kitchen is small, there simply isn't room for a lot of the clutter that keen cooks tend to accumulate, such as specialist utensils and equipment that are only used once in a while or gadgets that occupy valuable counter space. The same is true of food. If you open a cupboard and packets fall out, it's time to readjust your shopping habits. This is not to say you have to make do with the bare minimum, merely that it is crucial to keep on top of kitchen organization on a regular basis.

LEFT AND ABOVE Small kitchens have to make efficient use of every centimetre of available space. In practice, this generally means a fitted layout. Working out how to accommodate appliances and enough storage to cater for your needs can be tricky. Many retail outlets have their own design service. Here stainless steel appliances are combined with sleek white fitted units. The bold orange detailing adds a note of vitality.

RIGHT Located within an open-plan living area, this kitchen is handsome enough to be on constant view, arranged along the length of one wall. The dishwasher is concealed behind a décor panel.

THIS PAGE A charming, almost ad hoc kitchen is slotted into a corner under a sloping roof, allowing the character of the original structure to show through. White décor helps to give a sense of unity.

OPPOSITE A nicely judged mixture of contemporary and classic combines a traditional style table and chairs with modern units. The professional kitchen range incorporates its own stainless steel splashback.

A SENSE OF STYLE

Small kitchens don't mean you have to skimp on style. In fact, when space is restricted, you will be able to afford better materials for surfaces such as worktops or door panels, and better quality details such as handles. A beautiful counter in stone or solid hardwood will add a real touch of class.

One way of enhancing the sense of space is to stick to a relatively limited palette of materials for a homogeneous look. You can extend this strategy to its furthest reach by concealing appliances behind décor panels made of the same material used for drawer fronts and doors. Eliminating unnecessary detailing gives a streamlined look: flush panels rather than fielded ones, simple handles or chamfered drawer pulls, rather than elaborate designs.

But everything doesn't have to be hidden away – a kitchen that is as sterile as a laboratory is not a welcoming or inspiring place. Displays of glassware, plates or vegetables bring a sense of warmth and homeliness.

LIGHTING

A lot of what goes on in the kitchen is potentially hazardous – chopping with sharp knives, handling hot heavy pans, cooking over flames. To minimize the risk, it is essential to be able to see what you're doing, which means a good quality of light, both natural and artificial, and much brighter levels that you would require in a living area. If your kitchen is situated on a lower level or in part of your home that is naturally dark, you can borrow light from other areas by creating new openings or by bringing light down from above.

Fixed lighting makes sense in small kitchens, which are often fitted and fixed in layout. Ceiling-mounted spots, small downlights fitted to the base of wall-hung cabinets and similar adjustable light fittings can be positioned to target light at the hob and main preparation area. It is important to get the light angled correctly so that you are not working in your own shadow. Beware of glare: light is intensified when it bounces off shiny reflective surfaces such as glass and stainless steel.

LEFT An internal window over the kitchen sink provides borrowed natural light for the enclosed bathroom beyond. The circular disk in the middle is a mirror on the other side.

RIGHT A double pendant provides directs targeted illumination at a worktop, as well as creating gently diffused ambient lighting for the space as a whole. The wicker shades produce intriguing patterns of light and shade which are picked up by the reflective surfaces and finishes.

FIXED LIGHTING MAKES SENSE

IN SMALL KITCHENS, WHICH

ARE OFTEN FITTED IN LAYOUT

THIS PAGE A bespoke kitchen is neatly integrated into the space under the stairs. The elegant curve of the countertop makes an eye-catching and sculptural virtue of the siting.

Space-saving kitchens

- ■ Drawer dividers enable you to organize small items.

- ■ Moveable shelves allow you to organize items by height. Baskets keep like with like.

- ■ Racks on the back of doors are a good way of storing pan lids. Wall racks organize utensils in everyday use.

- ■ Pull-out or fold-down tops can serve as extra preparation space.

Kitchen units and appliances tend to come in standardized dimensions, so the typical height, breadth and depth of a dishwasher, for example, is about the same as a base cupboard. This both rationalizes production and makes it easier to assemble a fitted kitchen. But slimline or mini appliances are also available where space is really tight. These can be an option if they serve your needs effectively. Don't downsize, however, if that means compromising on basic efficiency and practicality.

More useful is to customize the interior of units. When you buy units, you are literally buying space. The problem is one size doesn't fit all. Where you need to find a home for large casseroles on the one hand and small spice jars on the other, adapting storage is the only answer.

ABOVE A deep Belfast sink is mounted within fitted units. Various accessories are available to enable you to make the most of modular storage space.

RIGHT A compact breakfast bar is out of the way of main kitchen traffic.

LEFT Eating areas in open-plan spaces need some kind of visual anchor to signal the shift of activity. Here this is provided by a pair of shelves, cantilevered from the wall, housing a display of decorative glassware.

THIS PAGE The separate dining room is definitely on the wane but many people still enjoy the sense of occasion it can provide. This generous expanse of glazing prevents a small dining room from feeling too claustrophobic.

EATING AREAS

Even in homes where the pressure on space is not so great, the separate dining room is not as common as it was. In large part this is down to the more inclusive nature of family life and a more informal approach to entertaining. Where they do exist, they often serve other functions some of the time. But this is not to dismiss the importance of having a dedicated place where meals can be shared with other family members and friends. Eating on a tray in front of the television isn't dining, it's refuelling.

The first decision you have to make is where to locate an eating area. In many homes, the dining room has been absorbed in an open-plan kitchen, or forms part of a single multipurpose space. Which option you choose depends on the layout of your home and the potential it offers for spatial change.

DEFINING THE SPACE

Where an eating area occupies part of a kitchen or general open-plan living space you need to signal the shift of activity in some way. A shared meal is a sociable occasion and should be relaxing, which entails some form of separation from other functions that the area must accommodate. Similarly, it is also essential to ensure that the table and chairs are situated away from the main traffic routes through the space, not simply to avoid the sense that you are eating in the middle of a station concourse, but also to avoid creating an unnecessary obstacle the rest of the time.

The basic shape and layout of the area in question might well suggest a natural location for an eating area. If the room is L-shaped, for example, the necessary spatial distinction is already built in. Alcoves and bay windows can also provide a feeling of intimacy and enclosure. Otherwise, think about siting the eating area so that it is anchored by a wall to one side of the main

LEFT The sideboard has made something of a comeback in recent years. Streamlined contemporary versions are available from major outlets, anonymous enough in style to provide storage space for table linen as well as CDs, media equipment and the like.

RIGHT This eating area is defined exclusively by furniture placement, with the backs of the armchairs defining the living space and the kitchen arranged exclusively along one wall.

living space. You can underscore the arrangement by decorating the wall in a different way, by picking it out in colour, for example, or cladding it in a contrasting material. A rug can also provide some spatial definition.

Views and sightlines are another aspect to take into consideration, particularly where the eating area is part of the kitchen. Here it is important to screen kitchen counters and preparation areas as far as possible – food is less appetizing when dirty pots and pans are on view. A long counter or peninsula will generally do the trick or, if you have enough room, consider placing the table at right angles to the kitchen area so you are not facing it.

FURNITURE AND LIGHTING

In the heyday of formal dining, dining room furniture was solid and imposing. Matching sets – often a sideboard as well as the table and chairs – were often highly finished and ornate. Today, tables and chairs tend to be

TODAY, TABLES AND CHAIRS
TEND TO BE SIMPLER AND
MORE ADAPTABLE

simpler and less specifically designed as dining furniture. This is a particular advantage if your eating area doubles up as place to work between mealtimes. By the same token, a plain low free-standing cabinet can house CDs and DVDs and other media along with the table linen and cutlery, and not look out of place in a multi-purpose room.

Tables with leaves that pull out or drop in are a good way of accommodating extra guests. Simple folding or stacking chairs can also serve as additional seating and be stored out of sight the rest of the time. Where space is really tight, you might consider a table top that folds down from the wall, or slides out from kitchen counter.

Lighting is a key element. Dimmer switches will allow you to lower the light to a level suitable for relaxed dining. Pendant fittings are a good way of lighting the table and creating a cosy intimate focus, and those on adjustable height pulleys offer greatest flexibility in terms of the mood they create. Make sure that the light source itself is not visible, especially on low pendants, so you avoid unpleasant glare as you look across the table.

LEFT An efficient use of space locates an eating area in a bay window, where it is not only out of the way but also benefits from natural light. The built-in bench seating is accessorized with cushions for additional comfort. The pendant light provides glare-free illumination.

RIGHT Even if you have only a limited amount of outdoor space, you can still take the opportunity to eat outdoors whenever the weather permits. Simple folding tables and chairs can be set up on terraces or balconies at a moment's notice and stored when not required.

BATHROOMS

Nowadays bathrooms have shrugged off their strictly functional image to become places where we retreat to pamper ourselves. Increasingly more and more money is being spent on fixtures and fittings that deliver a spa experience at home. When your bathroom is literally the smallest room, the challenge is to optimize the layout so you can still enjoy the same quality time despite the lack of space.

Early on in the planning process you need to make a number of key decisions. The first consideration is whether it is possible to increase the floor area, by moving a partition wall, for example. Even a small increase can make all the difference between a layout that is workable and one that is not. Then think about which features are essential. Could you make do with a shower

LEFT Small bathrooms call for a whole-hearted approach to decoration. Here slate tiling extends right up to the ceiling and encloses the bathtub. Contrasted with white paintwork, the look is crisp and graphic.

RIGHT Even if your bathroom is restricted in size, it can still provide a sense of retreat. Here a porthole window lights a shower that drains to the floor, and is separated from the sink by a glass screen. The moody blue décor lends a touch of drama.

THIS PAGE A half-height tiled partition separates the bathtub from the lavatory. The continuous mosaic surface gives a great sense of unity. Wall-mounted taps and fixtures are neater than conventional designs.

ABOVE LEFT Bathing areas can be slotted into sleeping areas if there is enough space. Both activities share the same basic need for privacy and retreat. Here a fully enclosed glass shower cubicle makes a minimal interruption to a bedroom.

ABOVE RIGHT Showers don't have to be regularly shaped. This walk-in shower, fully tiled in mosaic and screened by a translucent glass panel, occupies a triangular space.

instead of a tub? Do you really need a bidet? When small bathrooms are uncomfortable, it is often because the toilet is too close to the tub. Think about ways of arranging the layout so the toilet is separate or screened.

FIXTURES AND FITTINGS

Small bathrooms are the ultimate fitted spaces. If you find it difficult to plan the layout, many bathroom retailers and suppliers provide a design service and will help you come up with the best solution. All you need to do is measure the area and make a note of the position of existing servicing.

Take the time to research what is available. Compact ranges of fittings, specifically designed for small bathrooms, can be worth investigating. Many small bathrooms are also awkwardly shaped. Sinks and toilets are available in corner versions, which can help to make the most of a cramped or irregular floor plan. Tapered bathtubs can also be space-saving.

Visual neatness is another key strategy. Wherever possible opt for wall-hung sinks and toilets, which look lighter and less obtrusive than pedestal versions. Similarly, if you extend waterproof flooring into a walk-in shower and do without a shower tray, the effect will be more streamlined. Details matter — such as taps plumbed into the wall or heated towel rails that combine storage with ambient heating.

DECORATIVE STRATEGIES

A small bathroom can pack a big punch, decoratively speaking. All white — tiling, flooring and sanitaryware — is a classic solution, but it isn't the only one. Strong colour can be very effective in a small space. So can a bold contrast of material — wood panelling, for example, or smooth natural stone. If you opt for the fail-safe approach of tiling, make sure you tile the entire room from floor to ceiling so that walls read as continuous planes. Experiment with scale — mosaic is softer and more textural in appearance than tiles of a standard dimension, which can be a little clinical.

Fixed lighting makes sense in a small fitted space. Downlights recessed into the ceiling are a good solution here. Supplement with side-lighting to either side of the bathroom mirror to avoid harsh shadows on the face. Backlighting or under-lighting fixtures such as tubs and sinks can be atmospheric as well as space-enhancing. Mirror will multiply light and views and can really fool the eye. If you line facing walls with large sheets of mirror, a small bathroom will seem much less confined.

THIS PAGE Smaller sized bathrooms, particularly where they are fully internal, can be a little dark. One answer is to borrow light from adjacent areas. In this instance, a translucent glazed door allows light through without sacrificing privacy.

STORAGE

When your bathroom is small, you have to be ruthless about what you keep in it. An element of display is fine, particularly for products in attractive packaging; otherwise what you leave out on view should be in daily use.

Storage should be concealed wherever possible to keep clutter out of sight. If you opt for wall-hung fixtures, this may give you the opportunity to incorporate fitted storage for basic necessities such as cleaning products and spare toilet rolls within the dummy panel that hides the toilet cistern. With a little ingenuity, storage areas can also be slotted in underneath sinks and at either end of the bath. Bathroom cabinets come in a range of styles and sizes. Most useful are those that have a mirrored front; some also incorporate lighting for everyday routines such as shaving or putting on makeup.

BELOW LEFT Glazed doors and a long vertical window counteract any hint of confinement in a bathroom restricted in size. The wood panelling adds warmth where most of the surfaces are glass or metal.

BELOW RIGHT A successful strategy for a small bathroom is to choose wall-hung fixtures, such as this sink and lavatory.

THIS PAGE A shower fitting in the form of an extended pole is operated by wall-mounted controls. Minimal detailing enhances the sense of freedom that wet rooms can provide.

Wet rooms

- Underfloor heating makes wet rooms comfortable to use. This must be installed by a professional who has experience in this work

- Light fittings should be fully enclosed in waterproof housings to prevent any risk of water coming in contact with electricity.

- Wall-mounted taps and sculptural showerheads enhance the sense of space.

The fully waterproofed wet room is an ideal solution if you're short of space. In a wet room the shower is not enclosed in any way; instead it drains directly to the floor. Generally, toilets and sinks are wall-hung to keep the floor area clear. If there's room, you can also incorporate a bath. What a wet room does rule out, however, is much storage.

Wet rooms require careful construction. The floor must be laid so that water flows to the drain and does not form pools on the surface. The underlying structure of the walls and floor must be professionally waterproofed, either with a membrane or a bituminous layer, so there is no risk that damp can penetrate and cause damage. Surface materials must also be fully waterproof and, in the case of flooring, non-slip.

ABOVE Specialist secure construction prevents any risk of water penetrating surface finishes and affecting the structure of your home.

RIGHT Pebble mosaic makes a good non-slip surface that also massages bare feet.

LEFT A comfortable bed and good lighting is all you really need in a bedroom for it to serve its essential function. Think carefully about what else you put in the room – storage furniture is fine if it does not dominate, but fitted closets are often better.

RIGHT Bedroom décor should be all about comfort and reassurance. Here, the rich, deep colours of burgundy and plum used on the quilted bedhead and bedcover add a sense of visual warmth.

BEDROOMS

Bedrooms can be surprisingly minimal and still serve as peaceful retreats. Extensive floor area is not necessary, provided there is room for a bed of comfortable size and enough space around its perimeter for easy access. Nor do they need to be fully enclosed. Screening a small separate bedroom with translucent sliding doors or partitions of similar design can provide privacy without blocking light. In an open-plan space a mezzanine or a raised platform will give you the essential degree of separation for a decent night's sleep. If your bedroom or sleeping area has a low ceiling, a low-level bed can help you to feel less confined.

You can't save space in a bedroom by compromising on the size of the bed. Other pieces of furniture, however, may be more optional. For example, you can do without bedside tables if you build in a low shelf behind the bed

LEFT An uncurtained four-poster bed creates a room within a room. The palette of greys, grey-blue and neutrals provides a soothing backdrop for a good night's sleep.

RIGHT Attic spaces make good locations for bedrooms since limited head height is not an issue. Retreating to bed carries a special connotation when you are tucking yourself up under the eaves.

head to serve as a repository for books and glasses of water. Similarly, choose bedside lights that can be wall-mounted rather than table or floor lamps. Free-standing storage, such as wardrobes and chests-of-drawers, devour floor area and can make layouts more awkward unless they can be positioned out of the way in alcoves. Built-in storage solutions are much more workable.

DÉCOR AND LIGHTING

Most of the time we spend in the bedroom we are undressed, asleep and at our most vulnerable. Bedroom décor should be all about comfort, reassurance and warmth. Soft furnishings – curtains or fabric blinds at the window, carpet, rugs or natural fibre flooring underfoot – create a more intimate mood than hard surfaces and finishes. They are more insulating, too, and make the room quieter and warmer. Choose colours that make the

LEFT Low lines are particularly space-enhancing. This low-level bed makes the most of the room's volume. Clothes are stored in fitted cupboards with slotted doors to help air circulate.

RIGHT Accent colour provided by cushion covers, decorative objects and pictures adds vitality to white décor. A skylight set into the plane of the roof bathes the sleeping area in natural light.

most of whatever natural light your bedroom receives. A sunny room that faces south or west can stand cool neutrals and blues; a darker or more northerly aspect needs warmer shades. Restrict strong colour and insistent pattern to smaller details such as cushion covers and throws.

Bedrooms call for sensitive lighting. All too often, however, bedrooms feature central overhead lights, which are notorious for creating a deadened atmosphere. They also cause glare, which is even more apparent when you are lying in bed. If you must have an overhead fixture, put it on a dimmer switch and supplement with other diffused and angled light sources. Uplighting is a better way of providing ambient light in a bedroom.

In addition to background light, you will need more specifically targeted illumination on each side of the bed, especially if you like to read yourself to sleep. Shaded table lamps are perfectly adequate, though adjustable wall-mounted fixtures are more space-saving and flexible.

LEFT A dedicated dressing area can make sensible use of space. Here a wall of fitted cupboards, unobtrusively decorated to match the walls, houses a wardrobe and keeps the bedroom free of clutter.

BELOW LEFT Zippered plastic pouches that slide under the bed make good storage for jumpers, blankets and extra bedlinen.

BELOW RIGHT Modular storage boxes and containers house a great deal of bedroom clutter.

STORAGE

What puts the pressure on space in a small bedroom is the need for clothes storage. The neatest and most practical solution is to keep your wardrobe somewhere else in a scaled-down version of a dressing room. An adjoining hall or vestibule fitted with closets and drawers will keep the bedroom free from clutter and your wardrobe in better order. If such an approach simply isn't possible because of lack of suitable available space, you will need to incorporate storage areas into the bedroom without taking up too much floor area or drawing too much attention to them.

One useful storage area is under the bed. Specialist storage companies produce a range of products for under the bed storage, from flat plastic containers on wheels for shoes, to zippered pouches for bulky items such as jumpers and spare bedlinen. Otherwise, concealed fitted storage is the way to go – devote an entire wall or alcove to built-in cupboards and drawers and screen with flush doors painted the same colour as the walls.

LEFT Who gets the top bunk? When children are young enough to share a room, bunk beds are a classic solution. The great advantage is that they leave the floor as clear as possible for spreading out toys and games.

RIGHT These built-in platform beds are a variation on the bunk-bed theme. Set at right angles rather than stacked one on top of one another, they allow each child the same access to light and air.

CHILDREN'S ROOMS

Children may be smaller than adults but that does not mean they necessarily should be given a smaller bedroom. Up to the teenage years, what kids need is floor area – somewhere to play and spread out their toys. What's also required is plenty of storage space to keep toys, games, books and clothes in some kind of order. If there isn't enough room in their bedroom all that stuff will simply spread everywhere else. Colour-coded containers allow you to organize like with like or separate whose from whose.

Where siblings are sharing, it makes sense to maximize floor and storage area with space-saving beds. Bunk beds are a popular solution and almost all children love them. There is a wide range of designs on the market, or you can have them specially built. Single raised beds can also be space-saving. You can fit out the space underneath as a play or study area or devote it to storage.

THIS PAGE Translucent screens conceal a fitted wardrobe in an open-plan space. The effect is as handsome as any retail display.

Planning a wardrobe

■ Moveable shelves, drawers, containers, dividers, racks and rails will let you keep like with like and make the most of every available inch.

■ Double hang short items such as shirts, skirts and jackets. You need a depth of 60cm (2ft) for hanging.

■ Sliding or folding doors are more space-saving than conventional doors You can screen shelving with blinds if access is tight.

Clothes are one category of possession that really benefit from regular review. It's been estimated that most people wear only a fraction of they own – which effectively means that most of the space devoted to clothes storage is redundant. Take the opportunity to go through your wardrobe every so often and get rid of the bad buys, what doesn't fit or what is irreparably stained or damaged.

A key strategy is to rotate your wardrobe on a seasonal basis. Clean and repair your summer or winter clothing before you pack them away in mothproof bags. Concealed fitted clothes storage is by far the best solution if you are short of space. You can opt for off-the-peg fitted wardrobes or have closets and cupboards custom-built.

ABOVE Individual plastic storage boxes keep shoes in order. Other solutions include cloth tidies that hang from the door.

RIGHT A minimal hanging rail organizes coats and shoes for easy selection.

HOME OFFICE

If you are spending a significant amount of time on home-based work, you need to organize and equip a home office as carefully as you would a kitchen. Ad hoc arrangements may be all right for a while but they won't do much for your productivity or efficiency in the long term.

First, decide on a location. You will need some physical separation from the rest of the household to allow you to concentrate, a good quality of light, both natural and artificial, and dedicated storage space for files, equipment and other paraphernalia. Options for compact workstations include 'between' spaces, such as areas under the stairs, on large landings, or on a mezzanine level above the main living space. You can also set up a home office in part of a larger multi-purpose area and either separate it with a partition or build it into a storage wall so it can be closed off when not in use.

RIGHT Working from home gives you the opportunity to express your personal style. Retro or reclaimed wooden filing cabinets and plan chests deliver practicality and charm. With essential technology increasingly miniaturized, there is no need for the home office to be dominated by bulky electronic equipment.

LEFT A mezzanine level is a good location for a home office – separate from the rest of the household, but offering the type of sweeping view across space that is said to be an aid to concentration and creative thought. An adjustable task light provides the boost of illumination required for detailed work.

RIGHT Sliding panels keep the options open. When privacy is required, these timber floor-to-ceiling doors can be slid across to provide a psychological separation between home life and work.

FURNITURE AND EQUIPMENT

Working from home provides the opportunity to move away from the drab and utilitarian business style that characterizes most offices and express your personal taste. At the same time you must ensure you can work effectively and potentially for long periods without suffering back pain, RSI or any of the other stresses and strains that arise when working conditions are not ideal.

First and foremost, this means investing in a chair designed for desk use. Sitting in one position for too long is what causes back problems. Proper desk chairs that swivel and tilt allow you to make the constant subtle shifts of movement necessary to maintain healthy posture. As well as a decent chair and a stable surface set at the right height for writing or typing you will also need an adjustable task light to boost light levels specifically on the desktop. In the rest of the area, uplighting is one of the best ways of providing background light, particularly if you are working on screen.

Suppliers

FURNITURE

ADVANCE FURNITURE
2525 Elmwood Avenue, Buffalo,
NY 14217, USA
Toll-free: +1 800-477-2285
www.contemporaryfurniture.com

ALCOVE DESIGNS LTD
109 Lavender Hill
London, SW11 5QL, UK
+44 (0)20 7585 1481
www.alcovedesigns.com

ARAM
110 Drury Lane,
London WC2B 5SG, UK
+44 (0)20 7557 7557
www.aram.co.uk

B&B ITALIA
250 Brompton Road,
London SW3 2AS, UK
+44 (0)20 7591 8111
www.bebitalia.it

BEDEEZEE
+44 (0)800 012 2020
UK
www.bedeezee.co.uk
Bed suppliers; also supplies beds
with storage underneath.

CENTURY DESIGN
68 Marylebone High Street
London W1U 5JH, UK
+44 (0)20 7487 5100
(Andrew Weaving)
www.centuryd.com

THE CONRAN SHOP
Michelin House,
81 Fulham Road,
London SW3 6RD, UK
+44 (0)20 7589 7401

CRATE & BARREL
+1 800-967-6696
USA
www.crateandbarrel.com

FURNITURE.COM
USA
www.furniture.com

HABITAT
196 Tottenham Court Road,
London W1T 7LG, UK
+44 (0)20 7631 3880
or +44 (0)845 601 0740
for your nearest branch
www.habitat.net

HOME DEPOT
USA
Toll-free: +1 800 430 3376
www.homedepot.com

IKEA
255 North Circular Road,
London NW13 0QJ, UK
+44 (0)845 355 1141
www.ikea.co.uk
In the USA
Toll-free: +1 800-434-4532
www.ikea.com

KNOLL INTERNATIONAL
Toll-free +1 800-343-5665
USA
www.knoll.com

OPTIONS FURNITURE
+44 (0)845 375 2959
UK
www.optionsfit.com

POTTERY BARN
Toll-free: +1 888-779-5176
For stores across the US
www.potterybarn.com

SCP
135-139 Curtain Road
London EC2A 3BX, UK
+44 (0) 20 7729 1869
www.scp.co.uk

SKANDIUM
86-87 Marylebone High Street,
London W1U 4QS, UK
+44 (0)20 7935 2077
www.skandium.com

TARGET
1000 Nicollet Mall,
Minneapolis, MN 55403, USA
+1 612 304 6073
www.target.com

TWENTYTWENTYONE
274 Upper Street,
London N1 2UA, UK
+44 (0)20 7837 1900
www.twentytwentyone.com

WORKBENCH
Toll-free: +1 800-736-0030
USA
www.workbenchfurniture.com

STORAGE

BROOKSTONE
Toll-free: +1 800 846 3000
USA
www.brookstone.com

CALIFORNIA CLOSETS
1000 Fourth Street, Suite 800
San Rafael, CA 94901, USA
+1 415 256 8500
www.calclosets.com

CLOSET VALET
2033 Concourse Drive,
St Louis, MO 63146-4118
USA
Toll-free: +1 800-878-2033
www.closetvalet.com

CREATESPACE
+44 (0)1564 711 177
UK
www.create-space.com

EASYCLOSETS.COM
Toll-free +1 800-910-0129
USA
www.easyclosets.com

THE GENERAL TRADING
COMPANY
2 Symons Street, Sloane Square,
London SW3 2TJ, UK
+44 (0)20 7730 0411
www.general-trading.co.uk

The Holding Company
Unit 2 Finchley Industrial Estate
879 High Road
London N12 8QA, UK
+44 (0)20 8445 2888
www.theholdingcompany.co.uk

HOMEBASE
+44 (0)845 077 8888 for
branches across the UK
www.homebase.co.uk

HOMEOFFICEDIRECT.COM
Toll-free: +1 877 709 9700
USA
www.homeofficedirect.com

MUJI UK
www.mujionline.com
www.muji.co.uk

NEVILLE JOHNSON
Broadoak Business Park,
Ashburton Road West,
Trafford Park, Manchester
M17 1RW, UK
+44 (0)161 873 8333
www.nevillejohnson.co.uk

ORGANIZE-EVERYTHING.COM
Toll-free: +1 800 600 9817
USA
www.organize-everything.com

STACKS AND STACKS
1045 Hensley Street,
Richmond, CA 94801, USA
Toll-free: +1 800-761-5222
www.stacksandstacks.com

KITCHENS AND BATHROOMS

AGAPE
Via Po Barna, 69
46031 Corregio Micheli di
Bagnola, San Vito, Milan
Italy
+39 (0)376 250 311
www.agapedesign.it
Bathroom products and
accessories.

ALTERNATIVE PLANS
9 Hester Road, London
SW11 4AN, UK
+44 (0)20 7228 6460
www.alternative-plans.co.uk
Bathroom products, fixtures
and accessories.

AQUATECNIC
+44 (0)845 226 8293
UK
www.wetroom.info
Wide range of wetroom
products.

ARMITAGE SHANKS
Rugeley, Staffordshire
WS15 4BT, UK
+44 (0)154 349 0253
www.armitage-shanks.co.uk

ASTON MATTHEWS
141-147a Essex Road,
London N1 2SN, UK
+44 (0)20 7226 7220
www.astonmatthews.co.uk
Contemporary / traditional
bathrooms and accessories.

AVANTE BATHROOM
PRODUCTS
Thistle House, Thistle Way,
Gildersome Spur, Wakefield
Road, Moreley, Leeds
LS27 7JZ, UK
+44 (0)113 201 2240
www.avantebathrooms.com
Bathroom fixtures and fittings.

BATHSTORE.COM
+44 (0) 8000 232323 for a
catalogue.
UK
www.bathstore.com
Units, fixtures and accessories

BED, BATH AND BEYOND
Toll-free: +1 800 462 3966
Stores around the US.
www.bedbathandbeyond.com

BISQUE LTD
244 Belsize Road,
London, NW6 4BT, UK
+44 (0)20 7328 2225
www.bisque.co.uk
Large range of designer
radiators and towel rails.

BOFFI
via Oberdan, 70-20030
Lentate sul Seveso,
Milan, Italy
+39 (0)362 5341
www.boffi.com

BULTHAUP
37 Wigmore Street,
London W1U 1PP, UK
+44 (0)20 7495 3663
www.bulthaup.com
High quality contemporary
fitted and unfitted kitchens.

DORNBRACHT
Köbbingser Mühle 6. D-58640
Iserlohn, Germany
+49 (0)2371 433 0
www.dornbracht.com

IDEAL STANDARD
The Bathroom Works,
National Avenue, Hull
HU 4HS, UK
+44 (0)1482 346 461
for suppliers nationwide
www.ideal-standard.co.uk
Bathroom suppliers.

INSPIRATIONS BATHROOMS
www.inspirationsbathrooms.com
UK
+44 (0)845 262 4677
Bathroom fittings and fixtures.

JOHN LEWIS OF HUNGERFORD
Park Street, Hungerford,
Berks RG17 0EF, UK
+44 (0)1488 688 100
www.john-lewis.co.uk
Classic kitchens.

JOHNNY GREY
Fyning Copse, Fyning Lane,
Rogate, Petersfield, Hants
GU13 5DH, UK
+44 (0)1730 821 424
www.johnnygrey.com
Contemporary kitchens available
in UK and the US.

MAGNET
+44 (0)1535 661133 for
branches around the UK
www.magnet.co.uk
Fitted kitchens, appliances,
bathrooms, bedrooms and home
offices.

MFI
Branches around the UK
www.mfi.co.uk
Fitted kitchens, bathrooms and
bedrooms. Wide range of styles
from contemporary to classic to
country. Branches around the
UK. Design service available.

PLAIN ENGLISH
The Tannery, Combs,
Stowmarket, Suffolk
IP14 2EN, UK
+44 (0)1449 774 028
www.plainenglishdesign.co.uk
Shaker-style kitchens.

SHAKER
72/73 Marylebone High Street,
London W1U 5JW, UK
+44 (0)20 7935 9461
www.shaker.co.uk
Shaker-style kitchens and other
storage accessories.

SIEMATIC
www.siematic.com
Contemporary kitchen designs
available worldwide.

SMALLBONE
105-109 Fulham Road,
London SW3 6RL, UK
+44 (0)20 7581 9989
www.smallbone.co.uk
Classic kitchen designs.

VILLEROY & BOCH
Corporate Headquarters,
PO Box 1120, D 66688
Mettlach, Germany
+49 (0)686 481 0 and
www.villeroy-boch.com
In the UK
267 Merton Road, London
SW18 5JS, UK
+44 (0)208 871 4028
Manufacturers of bathroom
products – range designed by
Conran & Partners.

VOGUE (UK) LTD
+44 (0)1902 387000
www.vogue.co.uk
Heated towel rails & radiators.

WATERWORKS
469 Broome Street, New
York, NY 10013, USA
+1 212 966 0605
Bathroom fittings and fixtures in
the US.

DÈCOR, ACCESSORIES & LIGHTING

AMERICAN BLINDS,
WALLPAPER AND MORE
+1 800 575 8016
USA
www.decoratetoday.com

BORDERLINE
Unit 12, 3rd Floor
Chelsea Harbour Design Centre
London SW10 0XE, UK
+44 (0)20 783 3567
www.borderlinefabrics.com
Specializing in fabrics.

CONTEMPORARY CLOTH
Contemporary Cloth
PO Box 733, Willoughby,
Ohio 44094-0733, USA
+1 866 415 3372
www.contemporarycloth.com

DEBORAH BOWNESS
+44 (0) 7817 807504
UK
www.deborahbowness.com
Hand-printed wallpaper designs
featuring photographic images.

DESIGNERS GUILD
275/277 King's Road, London
SW3 5EN, UK
+44 (0)20 7893 7400 for
stockists
www.designersguild.com
Vibrant fabrics; flocked
wallpapers; paint collection.

DESIGNERPAINT
+44 (0)1323 430886
UK
www.designerpaint.co.uk

DULUX
+44 (0)870 444 1111
UK
www.dulux.co.uk
Extensive range of exterior and
interior paints.

EMERY & CIE
(Agnès Emery)
12 rue de Lausanne
10060 Brussels
Belgium
+32.2.513.5892
www.emeryetcie.com

FARROW & BALL
249 Fulham Road, London,
SW3 6HY, UK
+44 (0)20 7351 0273
www.farrow-ball.com
Manufacturer of traditional
paints and paper.

FEATURE RADIATORS
Bingley Railway Station
Wellington Street
Bingley, West Yorkshire
BD16 2NB, UK
+44 (0)1274 567789
www.featureradiators.com

THE HARDWOOD FLOORING
COMPANY
31-35 Fortune Green Road
London, NW6 1DU, UK
+44 (0)20 7431 7000
Hardwood flooring specialists.

LES EDITIONS DOMINIQUE
KIEFFER
8 rue Herold
75001 Paris
France
+33 (0)1 42 21 32 44
www.dkieffer.com

LIGHTFORMS
168 Eighth Avenue, New York,
NY 10011, USA
+1 212-255-4464
www.lightformsny.com
Lighting solutions.

THE LIGHTING CENTER LTD
240 East 59th Street, New York,
NY 10022, USA
+1 212 888 8380
www.lightingcenter-ny.com

LOOPHOUSE
88 Southwark Bridge Road,
London SE1 0EX, UK
+44 (0)20 7207 7619
www.loophouse.com
Custom handmade 100 per cent
wool rugs and related products
including wallpaper and
accessories.

MHS RADIATORS
UK
+44 (0)1268 546 700
www.mhsradiatiors.com

MULBERRY HOME
322 King's Road,
London SW3 5UH, UK
+44 (0)20 7623 3455 for
stockists
www.mulberry.com
Richly textured fabrics -
chenilles and velvets - as well
as plaids, tartans and checks.

THE NATURAL FLOORING
COMPANY
+44 (0)1952 825 459
UK
www.thenaturalflooringcompany.
com
Supply and installation of
natural flooring.

OSBORNE AND LITTLE
304 King's Road, London,
SW3 5UH, UK
+44 (0)20 7352 1456
www.osborneandlittle.com
Producers of bold ornamental
fabrics and papers since 1968.

ROGER OATES
l Munro Terrace, Riley Street,
London, SW10 0DL, UK
+44 (0)20 7351 2288
+44 (0)845 612 00722 for
stockists
www.rogeroates.com
Flatweaves, runners and Wilton
carpet.

PAPER AND PAINTS
4 Park Walk, London
SW10 0AD, UK
+44 (0)20 7352 8626
www.colourman.com
Colour-matching service; experts in
colour in historic buildings.

DOMINIQUE PICQUIER
10 rue Charlot, 75003 Paris, France
+33 (0)1 42 72 23 32
www.dominiquepicquier.com

THORSTEN VAN ELTEN
22 Warren Street, London,
W1T 5LU, UK
+44 (0)20 7388 8008
www.thorstenvanelten.com
Furniture, lighting and accessories.

URBAN OUTFITTERS
200 Oxford Street, London,
W1D 1NU, UK
+44 (0)20 7907 0800
www.urbanoutfitters.com
Fashion-led 'apartment' wares.
Stores across the US and UK.

USA WALLPAPER SHOWROOM
2419 E. Perkins Ave, Sandusky, Ohio
+1 800 573 5824
www.usawallpaper.com

WALLPAPERDIRECT
+44 (0)1323 430886
UK
www.wallpaperdirect.co.uk
Virtual wallpaper showroom.

WHITE SENSE (Martine Collinader)
Holländargatan 27
Stockolm 113 59, Sweden
+46.70.717.5700
www.mezzoshowroom.com

ZOFFANY
UK
+44 (0)8708 300350
www.zoffany.com
Famous fabric brand; also produces
www.upholster.com
upholstery magazine.

Architects & Designers

1100 ARCHITECT
435 Hudson Street
New York
New York 10014
USA
+1 (212) 645 1011
www.1100architect.com

ALEX VAN DE WALLE
Vlaamsesteenweg 3
1000 Brussels
Belgium
+32 (0)477 806 676
alex.vdw@swing.be

**ANDERSON MASON DALE
ARCHITECTS**
1615 Seventeenth Street
Denver
Colorado 80202
USA
+1 (303) 294 9448
www.amdarchitects.com

ANDREA TRUGLIO
75 via del Corso
00186 Rome
Italy
+39 06.361.1836

AZMAN ARCHITECTS
18 Charlotte Road
Shoreditch
London EC32A 3PB, UK
+44 (0)20 7739 8191
www.azmanarchitects.com

BUILDBURO
7 Tecott Road
London SW10 0SA, UK
+44 (0)20 7352 1092
www.buildburo.co.uk

CHERNER DESIGN
13 Crosby Street
New York
New York 10013, USA
+1 (212) 941 1300
www.chenerdesign.com

CLODAGH DESIGNS
670 Broadway
4th Floor
New York
New York 10012, USA
+1 (212) 780 5300
www.clodagh.com

FEATHERSTONE ASSOCIATES
74 Clerkenwell Road
London EC1M 5AQ, UK
+44 (0)20 7490 1212
www.featherstone-
associates.co.uk

FEBO DESIGNS
Lynne Fornieles
1 Foxcombe Cottages
South Harting
Petersfield
Hampshire GU31 5PL, UK
+44 (0)1730 82504

FOUGERON ARCHITECTURE
720 York Street
Suite 107
San Francisco
California 94110, USA
+1 (415) 641 5744
www.fougeron.co

GÉRARD FAIVRE
Avenue de la Republique
13810 Eygalières
France
+33 (0)4.90.95.98.50
www.gerardfaivre.com

GUY PETERSON FAIA
1234 First Street
Sarasota
Florida 34236
USA
+1 (941) 952 1111
www.guypeterson.co

**HALSTEAD DESIGNS
INTERNATIONAL**
515 E 72nd Street
Suite No 14L
New York
New York 10021, USA
+1 (212) 879 109

HEIBERG CUMMINGS DESIGN
9 West 19th Street
3rd Floor
New York
New York 10011, USA
+1 (212) 337 2030
www.hcd3.com

HENNIE INTERIORS AS
Thomles gate 4
0270 Oslo, Norway
+47 (0)22 06 85 86

J F DELSALLE
3 rue Seguier
75006 Paris, France
+33 (0)1 43 29 42 76
www.jfdelsalle.com

**JACKIE VILLEVOYE INTERIOR
ARCHITECTS**
(Breda, Netherlands)
+31 (0)765 60 11 00

LAURENT BUTTAZZONI
62 rue de Montreuil
75011 Paris, France
+33 (0)1 40 09 98 49

**MARC PROSMAN
ARCHITECTEN BV**
Overtoom 197
1054 HT Amsterdam
The Netherlands
+31 (0) 20 489 2099
www.prosman.nl

**MAXIME D'ANGEAC
ARCHITECTE**
41 rue Puchet
75017 Paris
France
+33 (0)1 53 11 01 82

MOOARC LTD
www.mooarc.com
+44 (0)20 7354 1729
+44 (0)1481 200021

NEXT ARCHITECTS
Weesperzijde 93
1091 EK Amsterdam
The Netherlands
+31 (0) 20 463 0463
www.nextarchitects.com

NICOLAS VIGNOT
6 rue Vaucouleurs
75011 Paris, France
+33 (0)6 11 96 67 69
http://n.vignot.free.fr

**OGAWA DEPARDON
ARCHITECTS**
137 Varick Street # 404
New York
New York 10013, USA
+1 (212) 627 7390
www.oda-ny.com

PAMPLEMOUSSE DESIGN INC.
USA
Delphine Krakoff
+1 (212) 980 2033
delphine@pamplemousse.com

PATRICK FRADIANI
Studio F
USA
+1 (773) 880 0450
www.studiof-design.com

RESISTANCE DESIGN
Eric Mailaender
11 Tompkins Place, No. 2
Brooklyn
New York 11231, USA
+1 (212) 714 0448
www.resistancedesign.com

RIOS ASSOCIATES INC
8008 West 3rd Street
Los Angeles, CA 90048, USA
+1 (323) 634 9220
www.rios.co

RUTHERFOORD, CHARLES
51 The Chase
London SW4 0NP, UK
+44 (0)20 7627 0182
www.charlesrutherfoord.net

STICKLAND COOMBE
ARCHITECTS
258 Lavender Hill
London SW11 1LJ, UK
+44 (0)20 7924 1699

STUDIO K O
7 rue Geoffroy l'Angevin
75004 Paris, France
+33 (0)1 42 71 13 92
komarrakech@studioko.fr
koparis@studioko.fr

THAD HAYES DESIGN INC
80 West 40th Street
New York
New York 10018, USA
+1(212) 571 1234

TODHUNTER EARLE
79-89 Lots Road
Chelsea Reach
London SW10 0RN, UK
+44 (0)20 7349 9999
www.todhunterearle.com

TRISTAN AUER
5a Cour de la Metairie
75020 Paris, France
+33 (0)1 43 49 57 20

USHIDA FINDLAY (UK) LTD
1 Fitzroy Street
London W1T 4BQ, UK
+44 (0)20 7755 2917
www.ushida-findlay.com

WELLS MACKARETH
ARCHITECTS
Unit 14
Archer Street Studios
10-11 Archer Street
London W1D 7AZ, UK
+44 (0)20 7287 5504
www.wellsmackareth.com

Acknowledgements

Photographers' credits

Ken Hayden
48-49 and 83.
Simon Upton
3 left, 4, 5, 6 above, 8-9, 16 right, 17-19, 21, 22, 25, 28-29, 31, 33, 35, 42-43, 55 above left, 56, 59, 60-61, 62-63, 68-70, 73 above, 78-79, 81 above right, 85, 88-89, 96-97, 101 right, 102-103, 109-111, 114-115, 118, 120-123, 126 and 128.
Frédéric Vasseur
Front jacket, 3 right, 13, 14, 20, 24, 29, 32, 37 left, 41, 45, 57, 58-59, 64-65, 75, 82, 87, 108, 129 and 132-135.
Luke White
26-27, 66-67, 81 above left & below right and 86.
Andrew Wood
1, 2, 3 centre, 6 below, 7, 11, 12, 15, 16 left, 23, 30, 34, 36, 37 right, 38-40, 44, 46-48, 50, 52-53, 55 above right & below, 63, 71-72, 73 below, 74, 76-77, 81 below left, 84-85, 90-95, 98-100, 101 left, 104-107, 112-113, 116-117, 119, 124, 127, 130 and 136-137.

Location credits

Front cover: Ben Cherner & Emma O'Neill's apartment in New York, designed by Emma O'Neill.

1-2 Weaving/Thomasson residence, London; 3 centre Dominique Kieffer's apartment in Paris; 3 right David Berg's house in Sweden; 4 designed by Stickland Coombe Architecture; 5 Martine Colliander of White Sense's apartment in Stockholm; 6 above a house in Oxfordshire designed by Todhunter Earle; 6 below Van Breestraat, Amsterdam, designed by Marc Prosman Architecten; 7 Tristan Auer's apartment in Paris; 8-9 designed by Stickland Coombe Architecture; 11 above left Weaving/Thomasson residence, London; 11 above right Tristan Auer's apartment in Paris; 11 below left Van Breestraat, Amsterdam, designed by Marc Prosman Architecten; 11 below right Alberdingh Thijmstraat, Amsterdam, designed by Marc Prosman Architecten; 12 Maxime & Athénais d'Angeac's home in Paris; 13 Ben Cherner & Emma O'Neill's apartment in New York; 14 James Falla & Lynn Graham's house in Guernsey, designed by James Falla at MOOArc; 15 Nipon apartment, New York, designed by Ogawa Depardon Architects; 16 left Van Breestraat, Amsterdam, designed by Marc Prosman Architecten; 16 right designed by Stickland Coombe Architecture; 17 designed by Stickland Coombe Architecture; 18-19 Yvonne Sporre's house in London, designed by J F Delsalle; 20 Nathalie Lété's house in Paris; 21 left Alex van de Walle's apartment in Brussels; 21 right Yvonne Sporre's house in London, designed by

J F Delsalle; 22 a loft apartment designed by Ushida Findlay; 23 Van Breestraat, Amsterdam, designed by Marc Prosman Architecten; 24 Nicolas Vignot's apartment in Paris; 25 Yvonne Sporre's house in London, designed by J F Delsalle; 26-27 Gérard Faivre's apartment in Paris; 28-29 designed by Stickland Coombe Architecture; 29 Dominique Picquier's house in Paris; 30 Princegracht, Amsterdam, designed by Next Architects; 31 Ben Langlands & Nikki Bell's house in London; 32 Patrizio Fradiani's house in Chicago; 33 a mountain retreat in Colorado, designed by Ron Mason; 34 Gerhard Jenne's house in London, designed by Azman Owens Architects; 35 a mountain retreat in Colorado, designed by Ron Mason; 36 Sarah Featherstone's kitchen in London; 37 left James Falla & Lynn Graham's house in Guernsey, designed by James Falla at MOOArc; 37 right Alberdingh Thijmstraat, Amsterdam, designed by Marc Prosman Architecten; 38-39 Tristan Auer's apartment in Paris; 40 Sarah Featherstone's kitchen in London; 41 above William Cumming's house on Long Island, designed by William Cummings at Heiberg Cummings Design; 41 below Patrizio Fradiani's house in Chicago; 42-43 a mountain retreat in Colorado, designed by Ron Mason; 43 a house in Oxfordshire designed by Todhunter Earle; 44 left Alberdingh Thijmstraat, Amsterdam, designed by Marc Prosman Architecten; 44 right Tristan Auer's apartment in Paris; 45 Dominique Picquier's house in Paris; 46 Tristan Auer's apartment in Paris; 47 left Gerhard Jenne's house in London, designed by Azman Owens Architects; 47 right De Stad, Amsterdam, designed by Next Architects; 48 Van Breestraat, Amsterdam, designed by Marc Prosman Architecten; 48-49 designed by Thad Hayes; 50 a house in London designed by Gordana Mandic of Buildburo; 51 left MHS Radiators Limited; 51 right Feature Radiators; 52-53 Sarah Featherstone's kitchen in London; 55 above left Ben Langlands & Nikki Bell's house in London; 55 above right Eric Gizard's apartment in Paris; 55 below left Van Breestraat, Amsterdam, designed by Marc Prosman Architecten; 55 below right Alberdingh Thijmstraat, Amsterdam, designed by Marc Prosman Architecten; 56 Ben Langlands & Nikki Bell's house in London; 57 Eric Mailaender's apartment in New York, designed by Eric Mailaender at Resistance Design; 58-59 Patrizio Fradiani's house in Chicago; 59-61 Martine Colliander of White Sense's apartment in Stockholm; 63 a house in London designed by Gordana Mandic of Buildburo; 64 Linda Barker's house in London; 65 Ben Cherner & Emma O'Neill's apartment in New York; 66-67 a New York penthouse loft designed by Clodagh Design; 68-69 a loft apartment designed by Ushida Findlay; 70 Reem Acra's apartment in New York; 71 Mark Badgley and James Mischka's New York apartment; 72 Shane/Cooper residence, New York designed by 1100 Architects; 73 above Agnès Emery's house in Marrakech; 73 below Gerhard Jenne's house in London, designed by Azman Owens Architects; 74 Mark Rios's home in Los Angeles; 75 Nathalie Lété's house in Paris; 76-77 a house in London designed by Lynne Fornieles of Febo Designs; 78-79 Alex van de Walle's apartment in Brussels; 81 above left a New York penthouse loft designed by Clodagh Design; 81 above right Martine Colliander of White Sense's apartment in Stockholm; 81 below left Weaving/Thomasson residence, Essex; 81 below right a New York penthouse loft designed by Clodagh Design; 82 James Falla & Lynn Graham's house in Guernsey, designed by James Falla at MOOArc; 83 designed by Jackie Villevoye; 84-85 Weaving/Thomasson residence, London; 85 Andrea Truglio's apartment in Rome; 86 a New York penthouse loft designed by Clodagh Design; 87 Reed & Delphine Krakoff's Manhattan townhouse, designed by Delphine Krakoff of Pamplemousse Design Inc.; 88-89 James Gager & Richard Ferretti's Pennsylvanian house; 90 a house in London designed by Lynne Fornieles of Febo Designs; 91 Amanda Halstead of Halstead Designs Intl; 92-93 Sarah Featherstone's kitchen in London; 94 Mark Rios's home in Los Angeles; 95 Alberdingh Thijmstraat, Amsterdam, designed by Marc Prosman Architecten; 96-97 Martine Colliander of White Sense's apartment in Stockholm; 98-99 Eric Gizard's apartment in Paris; 100 De Stad, Amsterdam, designed by Next Architects; 101 left a house in London designed by Lynne Fornieles of Febo Designs; 101 right Ivy Ross & Brian Gill's home in Galisteo; 104 a house in London designed by Lynne Fornieles of Febo Designs 105; Maxime & Athénais d'Angeac's home in Paris; 106 Weaving/Thomasson residence, Essex; 107 Weaving/Thomasson residence, London; 108 Harriet Maxwell Macdonald's apartment in London; 109 Martine Colliander of White Sense's apartment in Stockholm; 110 Michael Leva's house in Connecticut; 111 designed by Stickland Coombe Architecture; 112 Sally Mackereth & Julian Vogel's house in London, designed by Wells Mackereth; 113 left an apartment in Paris, designed by Studio KO; 113 right Fishman residence, Florida, interiors by Wilson Stiles, Sarasota, Florida, architect Guy Peterson FAIA; 114-115 a mountain retreat in Colorado, designed by Ron Mason; 116 Anne Fourgeron's house in San Francisco; 117 left Eric Gizard's apartment in Paris; 117 right Weaving/Thomasson residence, London; 118 James Gager & Richard Ferretti's Pennsylvanian house; 119 left Anne Fourgeron's house in San Francisco; 119 right Katy Barker's Paris apartment designed by Laurent Buttazzoni; 120-121 Michael Leva's house in Connecticut; 122-123 Martine Colliander of White Sense's apartment in Stockholm; 124 Andrea Truglio's apartment in Rome; 125 Weaving/Thomasson residence, London; 126 Weaving/Thomasson residence, London; 127 The Holding Company; 128 Mr & Mrs Sagbakken's cabin by the sea (Norway), interior design by Helene Forbes-Hennie; 129 David Berg's house in Sweden; 130 Shane/Cooper residence, New York designed by 1100 Architects; 131 The Holding Company; 132 Charles Rutherfoord & Rupert Tyler's London flat; 133 Nathalie Lété's house in Paris; 134-135 Nicolas Vignot's apartment in Paris; 136 Tristan Auer's apartment in Paris; 137 Van Breestraat, Amsterdam, designed by Marc Prosman Architecten.

Author's acknowledgements

I would like to thank all the team who worked on this book
for making it such a pleasurable experience: Jacqui Small,
Jo Copestick and Lesley Felce at Jacqui Small, and Sian Parkhouse,
Maggie Town and Nadine Bazar.